Peter Pearson's
Decorative Dublin

PETER PEARSON, artist and writer, has been passionately interested in his native city, Dublin, for most of his life. He has devoted many years, particularly during the 1980s, to working in a voluntary capacity to save historic buildings and districts. In 1985 he, along with a small group of architects and historians, campaigned the government to retain and revive the Temple Bar area, an action that has proven spectacularly successful.

As an artist he is widely known for his city paintings, which, at different times, have symbolised the decay, the change and the vigour of Dublin and show a love for its character and colour, its history and people. As a conservationist and art historian he has been a leading figure in developing public interest in the protection of the visual and built heritage of Ireland. To this end, he has collected a vast archive of salvaged artefacts from all over Dublin City and county. Many of the images in this book are taken from that archive, which bears witness to the piecemeal destruction of Dublin's architectural heritage.

Peter has been involved in numerous important publications: *Dun Laoghaire–Kingstown*, *Between the Mountains and the Sea*, *The Heart of Dublin*, *Dublin's Victorian Houses*, *The Forty-foot – a monument to sea bathing* and *The Royal St George Yacht Club*. All of his published work serves the very important and necessary purpose of recording and preserving the historic fabric of Dublin.

Peter Pearson's
Decorative
DUBLIN

PETER PEARSON
with photographs by Ian Broad,
Peter Pearson, Robert Vance
and David Davison
of Davison and
Associates

THE O'BRIEN PRESS
DUBLIN

Dedication
To Derek and Phyllis

First published 2002 by The O'Brien Press Ltd,
20 Victoria Road, Dublin 6, Ireland.
Tel: +353 1 4923333; Fax: +353 1 4922777
E-mail: books@obrien.ie
Website: www.obrien.ie
ISBN: 0-86278-784-X

British Library Cataloguing-in-Publication Data
Pearson, Peter, 1955-
Peter Pearson's Decorative Dublin
1. Decoration and ornament, Architectural - Ireland - Dublin
2. Dublin (Ireland) - Buildings, structures, etc.
I. Title II. Broad, Ian, ca. 1940-
720.9'41835

1 2 3 4 5 6
02 03 04 05 06 07

The O'Brien Press receives
assistance from

Editing, typesetting, layout and design: The O'Brien Press Ltd
Front cover photograph: Robert Vance
Printing: Eurolitho, Milan (Italy)

Picture Credits

Copyright for photographs, except those by Ian Broad and Robert Vance,
belongs to the individual photographer. Photographs of the Pearson Archive were taken by David
Davison at the behest of the Irish Georgian Society. The author and publisher would like
to thank the following for permission to reproduce images:

Key: t = top; m = middle; b = bottom; A = all; L = left; R = right

IAN BROAD: back cover: stained glass, roundel, doorknocker, Mansion House, front flap (t), pages 1, 3, 6 (both), 7 (mR, b), 10 (A), 11 (t, bL), 12 (m), 14-15 (A), 16, 18 (t, m), 21 (m), 23 (b), 24 (A), 25 (R), 28, 43 (m), 47 (bR, L), 51 (t, m), 52-53 (A), 56-57 (A), 58 (A), 59 (bL), 65 (t), 66, 67 (t), 68 (bR), 69 (t, bR), 74 (A), 75 (tR, L), 76-77 (A), 79 (A), 80 (t, m), 81 (A), 82-83 (A), 84, 93 (t), 104 (bL), 105 (t), 106 (m, b), 108 (A), 109 (t), 112 (b, two pics), 113 (A), 115 (A), 118 (A), 119 (m, b), 120 (t), 121 (first m), 125 (tL), 138 (A), 139 (b), 141 (A), 142 (bL), 143 (bm, bR), 144 (bR), 145 (tR and bL), 146 (bR), 147 (t, mR, bR), 148 (t, m, bR), 149 (tL, m, bR), 150-151 (A), 152 (bR), 153 (bR); DAVID DAVISON: back cover: coal plate, tile, fanlight, pages 7 (t, far L), 28 (tL), 31 (bR), 37 (b), 38 (b), 39 (m), 40 (far L, b), 41 (far R), 42 (t), 44 (collection of four small covers), 50 (A), 51 (b), 59 (t), 86 (b), 87 (A), 88 (A), 94 (A), 95 (b), 96-97 (A), 104 (R), 105 (b), 132 (b, L-R, various tiles), 134, 135 (t), 142 (tL), 153 (tR); DAVID MEEHAN: page 72;

NESSA O'CONNOR: page 155 (tL); PETER PEARSON: pages 4, 5, 11 (bL, bR), 12 (b), 13 (t), 19 (A), 20 (A), 21 (t), 22 (A), 23 (t), 25 (L), 26-27 (A), 29 (A), 30 (A), 31 (tR), 32-33 (A), 34-35 (A), 36, 37 (t), 38 (t, m), 39 (t, b), 41 (tL), 43 (bR), 44 (t, b), 45 (A), 46, 47 (t), 54 (b), 55, 59 (bR), 61 (A), 62-63 (A), 64, 65 (b), 67 (b), 68 (tR, L), 69 (tL), 70-71 (A), 75 (bR), 78 (t, m), 80 (bL), 85 (A), 86 (t L), 89, 92 (m, b), 93 (b), 95 (tR), 99, 100-101 (A), 104 (tL), 106 (tL), 107 (A), 110, 111 (tL), 112 (t, m), 114 (A), 116-117 (A), 119 (t), 120 (b, two pics), 121 (t, second m, b), 122-121 (A), 124, 128 (tR), 126-127 (A), 128-129 (A), 130, 132 (t, first m, second m), 133 (A), 135 (b), 136-137 (A), 140 (m, b), 142 (bR), 143 (bL), 144 (t, m), 145 (bR), 146 (tL), 147 (bL), 148 (bL), 149 (tR), 152 (t, m, bL), 154, 155 (bR, L), 156-157 (A), 158; ANDREW SMITH: page 92 (tL); ROBERT VANCE: endpaper image; front cover; back cover: metope, campanile, sculpted head, coat of arms, the Casino, pages 8, 12 (t), 13 (b), 21 (b), 42 (b), 43 (t, bL), 48, 54 (t), 60, 90, 92 (tR), 98, 102, 111 (R), 139 (t), 140 (t), 144, (bL) 155 (tR).

Acknowledgements

The production of this book was very much a collaborative effort, and special thanks must go to Ian Broad, Íde Ní Laoghaire, Rachel Pierce and Emma Byrne for their great dedication in photography, deciphering handwriting, editing and layout.

While paper records, articles and books can provide a useful background picture, much can be learned about decorative Dublin from a hands-on examination of the artefacts themselves and from talking to craftspeople and designers.

The contribution of Ian Broad, who took most of the new photographs and revisited so much of the city he knows so well, must be particularly noted. I am also indebted to Robert Vance for his artistic photographs of Dublin, one of which is featured on the cover. The assistance of David Davison and the Irish Georgian Society in photographing architectural fragments must also be specifically acknowledged, and also the work of Kevin Mulligan in cleaning and restoring many artefacts.

I am also grateful to Daniel Gilman for the use of various pictures and as a source of inspiration, and to the late Nessa O'Connor and her family, Michael and Marie-Ann Gorman, Hugh and Maureen Charlton, the Tomkin family, Mrs Mary Kelleher of the RDS, David Griffin and the staff of the Irish Architectural Archive, Denis McCarthy of Dublin Castle, Desirée Shortt and Andrew Smith.

I would like to thank the staff of the Dublin Civic Trust, especially its Director, Geraldine Walsh, and Mairéad Ní Chonghaile, Emmeline Henderson, Julie Craig, Olwyn James and Katriona Byrne for their excellent street studies of Camden Street, Thomas Street, South William Street, Capel Street and Pearse Street.

I would particularly like to thank all those people, both owners of houses and staff of public buildings, who readily facilitated the taking of photographs, including Bewley's Café, Grafton Street and Bewley's Hotel, Ballsbridge; the Ulster Bank, College Green; the National Museum; the National Library; the Irish Museum of Modern Art; the National Gallery of Ireland; Newman House; Dublin Corporation's Civic Museum and Mansion House; the Rotunda Hospital; Belvedere College; the Airfield Trust; Gort Mhuire, Ballinteer; St Patrick's Hospital; St Edmondsbury; St Werburgh's Church; the Bank of Ireland, College Green; Marsh's Library; the National University of Ireland; the Ombudsman's Office; the Office of Public Works and Dúchas, the Heritage Service; and the Royal Dublin Society.

A Note on Sources

Particular thanks must also go to Ian Lumley, Lindon Page and Charles Duggan who prepared the important Dublin Civic Trust exhibitions on fanlights, windows, doors, ironwork and brick. Ada Longfield's article, 'Old Wallpaper in Ireland', published in the JRSAI in 1948, provided the first overview of this interesting subject. I also wish to credit Susan Ruantree's unpublished thesis on brick-making in Ireland, as well as various articles published in the *Irish Arts Review*, including 'Irish Period Wallpapers', by David Skinner (1997), 'Ironsmith Timothy Turner', by Miriam O'Connor (1996) and 'The work of wood carver Carlo Gambi', by Patricia McCarthy (2002). The original *Georgian Society Records (1909-1913)* and the *Bulletin of the Irish Georgian Society* have also been most useful.

Derry O'Connell's *The Antique Pavement* (1975) and Matt Byrne's *Our Granite Pavements* (1987), both published by An Taisce, were also pioneering works. Other most useful reference books include: Peter Costello, *Dublin Churches* (1989); Maurice Craig, *Dublin 1660-1860* (1952); CP Curran, *Dublin's Decorative Plasterwork* (1967); Joe Curtis, *Times, Chimes and Charms of Dublin* (1992); Jim Fitzpatrick, *Three Brass Balls* (2001); Nicola Gordon-Bowe, *Harry Clarke* (1979); David Griffin and Caroline Pegum, *Leinster House* (2000); Desmond Guinness, *Georgian Dublin* (1979); Harbison, Potterton and Sheehy, *Irish Art and Architecture* (1978); James Howley, *The Follies and Garden Buildings of Ireland* (1993); Roisin Kennedy, *Dublin Castle Art* (1999); Frank Keohane, *Period Houses – A Conservation Guidance Manual* (2001); Paul Larmour, *The Arts and Crafts Movement in Ireland* (1992); Pat Liddy, *Dublin, A Celebration* (2000); Patrick McAfee, *Irish Stone Walls* (1997); Joseph McDonnell, *Irish Eighteenth-Century Stuccowork and its European Sources* (1991); Edward McParland, *Public Architecture in Ireland, 1680-1760* (2001); Meenam and Clarke, *The Royal Dublin Society, 1731-1981* (1981); Jane Meredith, *Around and About the Custom House* (1997); Peter Pearson, *Between the Mountains and the Sea* (1998); Peter Pearson, *Dun Laoghaire–Kingstown* (1981); Peter Pearson, *The Heart of Dublin* (2000); Nessa Roche, *The Legacy of Light, A History of Irish Windows* (1999); Sambrook and Gray, *Fanlights – A Visual Architectural History* (1990); John Sambrook, *Fanlights* (1989); John Sproule, Irish Industrial Exhibition catalogue (1854); Williams, Jeremy, *A Companion Guide to Architecture in Ireland, 1837-1921*. In addition, old trade catalogues have proven to be a very useful point of reference for ironwork and other materials, and these include: Baxendale's of Capel Street and The Building Trades Standard catalogues.

Finally, very special thanks must go to Phil, Adam and Jerome for giving time and space for the making of *Decorative Dublin*.

Contents

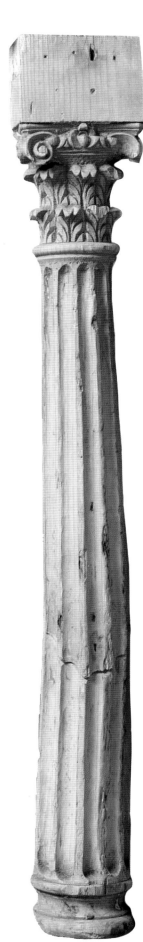

Introduction

The great European traditions of classical and medieval style, which influenced so much of our visible inheritance, have been abandoned in the last half-century to new, largely functional styles. There is a sense in which decoration is today considered *passé*, belonging to times past, part of the irrelevant nostalgia for things old. Many designers, whether in architecture, interiors or everyday objects, would be embarrassed to use decoration, except perhaps in an abstract way. The aim of this book is to celebrate the wonderfully rich array of decorative features that is waiting to be discovered in Dublin's architecture and streetscapes, from railings, fanlights, stone carving and plasterwork to stained glass, terracotta, marble mantelpieces and much more besides. The great achievement of the craftsmen who produced these features is that many of them form an integral part of buildings which have become much-loved landmarks in the city. One of the purposes of this collection is to highlight, through pictures, the beauty of such original details and to provide authentic examples, giving dates and makers' names, where known.

Though these decorative features will be examined mainly by material, such as wood, iron or stone, such is the variety of shape and form that is to be found that other special categories, such as weathervanes, coats of arms, fountains and lettering on buildings, have also been included. The elements described and illustrated reflect quite a personal choice, and it may be that some significant aspects have been overlooked, or given scant attention, while other subjects have been indulged. There are also some features, such as doors, door surrounds, or staircases, which appear more than once in the book. This is because a variety of materials was used in their construction.

Opposite page: Christ Church Cathedral, reconstructed in 1875, has a rich store of decorative detail in stone, wood, iron, tile and glass.

Most of the materials featured lend themselves to decoration and have the capacity to be painted, shaped, moulded or carved into some permanent ornamental form. These include cast and wrought iron, brick, terracotta and tiles, timber and wood carving, masonry, stone carving and stone sculpture, internal and external plasterwork, wallpaper and mosaic. Though it might have been interesting to explore and display, for instance, animals as a theme in all the various materials, the book is for the most part organised by style and type of ironwork and stonework. Although some subjects, such as lettering, employ almost every material to great effect. By attempting to sample so many of the pleasures of 'decorative Dublin', it was inevitable that there would neither be enough time to research each subject fully, or enough space to illustrate fully the complete range of examples. It is clear that a whole book could be dedicated to any one of the topics covered.

To some, the word 'decorative' implies superfluous, useless or unnecessary. But decoration was seldom applied in such a way. For instance, the low-relief ornament on a circular coal plate serves two purposes. Firstly, it provides a grip so that pedestrians will not slip on it when walking on the footpath after a shower of rain. Secondly, its patterns — usually a geometric arrangement of stylised leaves — serve to distinguish the opening to a particular coal cellar. Likewise, a fancy cupola or tower crowning the

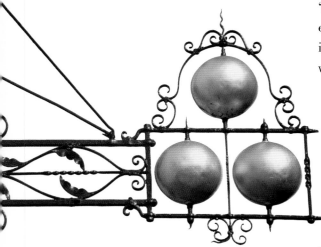

summit of a building is often much more than a mere ornamental afterthought, and can act as a ventilator to draw fresh air into a building, as a decorative means to hide a water tank, to display a public clock, or even to indicate wind directions with a weathervane. Some features, such as clock towers and weathervanes and indeed cupolas, provide the city with much-needed landmarks. Others are symbolic and proclaim the occupant's status, or hint at the nature of the profession that is carried on there, perhaps through a piece of sculpture. The Irish House, a Victorian pub on Wood Quay, left no doubt as to the politics of its owner with its decorated plaster façade of round towers, wolfhounds and Daniel O'Connell making a speech. Decorative elements were rarely, if ever, purely decorative.

At its simplest level, decoration is pattern-making. While many patterns are, of course, abstract, such as the Greek Key, the majority are inspired by nature and have their origins in the study of plants, leaves and flowers, or in animal or human forms and shapes. Patterns are formed by repeating an image, whether represented realistically, like a carved leaf, or stylised, like the classical egg-and-dart moulding. A favourite device in Romanesque architecture was the chevron moulding, a repeated dog-tooth type pattern, which later became much used in the nineteenth century for brick cornices and arched doorways.

But if ornament and pattern are simply the result of repetition of natural or abstract shapes, why does it seem so irrelevant in modern architecture? Why not devise new, contemporary ornament appropriate to specific buildings? One of the reasons why good decoration vanished from buildings in the twentieth century was that new materials, such as concrete, glass and steel were factory-produced and did not lend themselves to any form of hand-

made ornament. Also, the cost of hand-crafted details, such as cut stone or wrought iron, steadily increased as the requisite skills began to die out. Lastly, and perhaps most importantly, from the 1930s onwards popular taste dictated that ornament as it had been understood in previous centuries was outmoded, that form should express function.

The severity of the functional style brought about an eventual backlash in the late twentieth century in the form of ridiculous neo-Georgian, or Tudor-revival concoctions designed to feed on nostalgia, but which was at the same time oblivious to the appropriateness of the style and the correctness of its use.

The original principles of classical architecture were laid down in ancient Greece and Rome and evolved from the building of majestic temples, such as the Parthenon in Athens. Afterwards the Romans applied this architectural language to a host of other structures, such as aqueducts, amphitheatres and archways.

Classicism all but disappeared in the Middle Ages, but was reinvented during the Italian Renaissance and once again found new life in the eighteenth century, especially in Britain and Ireland where it was adapted to a wide range of building types, including houses, churches, public buildings, entrance gates, doors and shopfronts. The complex rules of classical proportion and decoration were altered and reshaped by different designers in different generations. For instance, in 1754 Robert Adam and his brother James travelled to Split to see the excavated palace of the Roman emperor Diocletian, on the bay of Aspalathos. The Adams's own published designs, many of them derived directly from these Roman sources, were to have a huge influence on architecture and decoration not only here

This page
Top: A late nineteenth-century terracotta panel with monogram from the North Wall Hotel in Dublin Port.
Right: The Iveagh Markets in Francis Street, built in 1902, is decorated with a series of keystone heads representing the major trading nations of the world. This example represents North America.
Below: The post office in Ballsbridge demonstrates the use of terracotta as an enduring medium for lettering.

Opposite page
Top: A ceramic overdoor and door surround in the National Museum is typical of the late Victorian taste for Italian style.
Bottom: The attractive octagonal clock tower of Dr Steevens's Hospital houses the oldest public clock in Dublin.

but in Britain and America, too.

The influence of the Adams brothers was very significant, but other noted designers and writers also had a profound effect on the history of architectural ornament. In the nineteenth century, for example, the English designers Augustus Welby Pugin and William Morris, along with writers like John Ruskin, played a significant part in promoting different Gothic and medieval revivals, which would be the dominant styles in Victorian times. William Morris, in particular, lamented the availability of mass-produced ornament in tiles, wallpaper and ironwork in the nineteenth century, and argued strenuously for the reinstatement of original, artistic designs derived from the study of nature and handcrafted artefacts.

However, while nothing can compare with an original piece from, say, a stone carver, blacksmith or artist, it is really only poor mass-production that should be condemned. Today we enjoy the mass-produced terracotta details which embellish so many Victorian houses, and many people cherish

the mass-produced cast-iron fireplaces of that period. It is tempting to argue that without the benefit of mass-production and the choices it brought, our Victorian houses would be very much less interesting. But it was, in fact, the harmonious marriage of the two – the mass-produced and the original – that made Dublin's old houses unique. Alongside the mass-produced items were, for example, the hundreds, or possibly thousands of fanlights which embellished the front doors of so many eighteenth- and early nineteenth-century houses in the city and county, and which were all individually handcrafted. While identical fanlights are sometimes found, as for instance in parts of Rathmines, it is rare to find two of the exact same dimension and pattern.

The staggering quantity of decorative detail that was applied to houses, in particular, is a tribute to the generations of largely forgotten craftsmen and tradesmen who made and fitted such features, be they iron railings, stonework, joinery, or plasterwork. Collectively, the legacy they created and left behind is a wonderful heritage that is a joy to the eye.

Most of the makers of the objects and decorative details featured in the following pages are unknown to us, as very few records of any kind exist that might indicate their names, or where they lived and worked. Who made the delicate fanlights, cut the stone pillars, or carved the marble mantelpieces of Dublin's Georgian homes? We shall probably never know. The guilds in Dublin once controlled some trades, such as blacksmiths, bricklayers, stonemasons, joiners and carvers, but their records do not tell us much about their work, or for whom they worked.

The names that are known to us are those of the most distinguished craftsmen, and lists from street directories and newspaper advertisements can throw some light on their activities. And, of course, we have better knowledge of later periods. The new technologies of the Industrial Revolution meant that many mass-produced articles could be stamped with the maker's name and as a result most Victorian bricks and tiles can be identified as being from a specific factory or workshop.

In a few, rare cases, such as in the building of the Rotunda Hospital, or

This page
Above: Victorian stained glass was often richly coloured and representational, like this image of Leonardo Da Vinci in the National Library.
Below right: The strikingly large dome and cupola of Our Lady of Refuge Church in Rathmines is a landmark in the Dublin skyline.
Opposite page
Top: One of the graceful muse figures, modelled in plasterwork by the La Francini brothers, which decorate the walls of the Apollo room in 85 St Stephen's Green.
Bottom: The clock tower from St Anne's Park, Raheny, constructed in the 1870s, was designed as a garden entrance in the private estate of the Guinness family.

parts of Trinity College, records do survive and provide the names of ironworkers and stuccodores and the amounts they were paid. Though it was not the norm for craftsmen to sign their work, there are valuable exceptions. During the demolition of a house in Parnell Square in the 1980s, a timber pilaster from the hallway was found to have stamped on the back the name of joiner, Mack, whose descendants became noted furniture-makers in Dublin in the nineteenth century. In another instance, while houses on Eccles Street were being dismantled, the back of one of the stair brackets was found to have the following message from its maker: 'For the Lord Mayor's (house), 2 dozen, signed Arthur Mooney.' The glaziers who worked on Dublin's City Hall left their signatures for posterity on the eighteenth-century glass high up in the windows of the dome (*see* illustration, p.61).

Some epochs in the history of Dublin's decorative art are badly represented. For instance, there is little to show for the medieval period or the seventeenth century. Likewise, very little remains of the modern movement of the twentieth century and examples of Art Nouveau buildings are also few, although it is possible to find a good number of cast-iron fireplaces with tiles and stained-glass windows which represent the latter style. It is not surprising that there is a predominance of eighteenth-century classical features, as Dublin was once considered to be the most impressive Georgian city after London. In their own time the great architects, like Edward Lovett Pearce and James Gandon, introduced impressive architecture to Dublin, which would influence successive generations.

It is now widely recognised that it was unfortunate, if not sometimes tragic, that so many old buildings were destroyed over the last thirty years, with the loss of much fine craftsmanship in stone, brick, iron, joinery and plaster, not to mention carved detail, mosaic, painted ceilings and stained glass. The destruction of traditional timber sash windows, along with their old glazing, has been so thorough and systematic that only a small fraction of original windows now remains in this country.

The original and authentic features are generally more pleasing to the eye and are more enduring. So, while it is possible to replace iron railings with exact replicas, it is very difficult to get the same quality of rust-resistant iron as that used 200 years ago. And while it is possible to make excellent wooden copies of Georgian windows and reglaze them in the same manner, it is very expensive and difficult to find the old hand-made glass that was originally used. Little by little the decorative detail from the past will slip away unless it is looked after and cherished. Some buildings are being demolished and ornamental details are being overlooked and consigned to neglect. This book is an attempt to preserve not only the beautiful minutiae but also the larger decorative detail of Dublin's unique cityscape.

Ironwork

Since the first primitive efforts of the Iron Age, people have recognised the potential of iron as a strong and enduring material that could be used for decorative as well as functional purposes. We often tend to think of iron as being a heavy and perhaps clumsy material, yet it is the very delicacy of, for example, an iron balcony, when contrasted with the solidity of brick, stone or plastered walls, that makes it work so well as a decorative medium. Most decorative ironwork has a function, though it may well be disguised. The ornamental weathervane tells the direction of the wind, a delicate balcony extends internal space out beyond the window, and eye-catching railings mark a boundary.

Ideal for security, iron has been used for gates, railings and even doors for many centuries. But it is also extremely versatile and can be worked locally by a blacksmith, or can come in a wide variety of ready-made shapes and styles available from catalogues from places further afield, such as the great iron manufacturers of Scotland and England. This versatility means that decorative ironwork can take many forms and can be adapted for such objects as bootscrapers, lamp standards and signs, as it is in Kildare Street, where the name of the National Museum appears over the entrance gate.

Ironwork comes in two forms: wrought and cast. Wrought iron is a pliable material that can be heated up and forged on the anvil, beaten into a multiplicity of functional joints and ornamental designs. Cast iron, by contrast, must be melted into a liquid and then poured into a mould. The resulting metal is more brittle than wrought iron and can be shattered by a blow from a hammer. However, it has the advantage of being reproducible in an unending variety of decorative details and structural members. In the later eighteenth and early nineteenth centuries cast iron offered a greater range and economy than ever before.

Opposite page: The highly ornamental gates at the entrance to the Ulster Bank on College Green are original to the impressive and monumental building, which was designed by Sir Thomas Drew. They date from 1891 and are typical of the lavish late Victorian taste. The makers are recorded as J&C M'Gloughlin.

In terms of ornament both wrought iron and cast iron have many applications. For instance, four decorative statues support lamps in front of the Shelbourne Hotel at St Stephen's Green, lion masks hide the seams of gutters on a Victorian house, solid discs of cast iron decorated with oak leaves act as covers in the footpath for coal cellars, and delicate honeysuckle motifs are woven into Georgian balconies.

Dublin has a large amount of historic ironwork intact, especially compared to English towns and cities, which lost so much of it during the two World Wars when railings were melted down and reconstituted as weapons. It is hard to say how much of all this ironwork was produced here in Ireland, or if much of it was imported from Britain and Scotland. Many smaller items, such as firegrates, were certainly imported while larger objects, such as gates, were generally made locally. A significant number of items are stamped with their maker's name, or bear a small plate as a form of advertisement. Maker's names were discreetly stamped into the stiles of gates, or appeared at the bottom of uprights, or of street lamps and were usually much overpainted.

In the eighteenth century the use of wrought iron was largely confined to street furniture, and an impressive array of such items can still be seen in Dublin. Useful pieces necessary for security and lighting, such as railings, gates and oil and gas lamp standards, are widely in evidence, along with postboxes, coal-hole covers, gates and railings, chains and bollards. Cast-iron bollards line the quays where they were used for tying up ships, but they were also employed to prevent access or damage to

Above: The wrought-iron scroll, probably made in the late nineteenth century, which supports the hanging sign of Greene's Bookshop is one of the most elaborate in Dublin.

Right: This doorknocker, called 'The Wellington', dates from the early nineteenth century. The hand holding the wreath is said to be an emblem of the defeat of Napoleon.

Below right: This very typical photograph of O'Connell Street (then Sackville Street), taken in about 1900, shows part of Dublin's principal thoroughfare serviced and ornamented by various examples of metalwork – functional, decorative and sculptural. The tall poles, with their gantries or arms decorated by ironwork scrolls, carried electric power for the trams, while the ornamental gas lamp standards illuminated the street at night. To the right is one of four symbolic bronze angels, which support the base of the O'Connell Monument. The impact of such ironwork as street furniture can be appreciated.

Above: A cast-iron porch and canopy at Beechpark, Castleknock, County Dublin. The application of decorative panels of ironwork for balconies, porches and verandas was developed in the late Georgian period and reached its peak in the period 1800–1830. The delicate white-painted trellis of patterned ironwork could be used to create a focal point on a building, or to accentuate an architectural feature, such as double doors leading into the garden. Similar verandas were sometimes constructed in timber, but cast iron has generally proven more durable.

Right: A very unusual and highly decorated tripod oil lamp standard from the front of St Stephen's Church, otherwise known as the Pepper Canister, on Upper Mount Street.

Below: At Bewley's Hotel, Ballsbridge, cast iron was used for a wide variety of applications, such as in this Victorian garden seat.

Bottom: A detail of a nineteenth-century cast-iron window from the foundry of Sheridan & Co., Bridgefoot Street, Dublin.

public buildings by vehicles, examples include the bollards outside the GPO and those near the Parnell Monument on O'Connell Street. Drinking fountains provide a good illustration of the versatility of iron and the level of craftsmanship achieved. They were usually made so that the water issued from the mouth of a lion, and often had an iron cup attached to the fountain by a chain. Some of the most beautiful eighteenth-century ironwork in Dublin, including gates and lamps, was illustrated and described in the early 1900s in the *Georgian Society Records*.

Another item of street furniture, shop signs, once came in a wide variety of forms, but those made of iron, which were hung above the premises, were by far the most effective form of advertising. Among the relatively few that have survived in the streets of the city is the famous three brass balls of the pawnbroker, Kearn's of Queen Street. It displays a fine wrought-iron sign, the scrollwork of which supports the gilded balls. Another majestic pawnbroker's sign may be seen on the premises of P Carthy in Marlborough Street, near the Pro-Cathedral. The origin of this sign is obscure, with some attributing it to the achievements of the Medici family in Italy. A more likely source is the fact that the moneylenders of Lombardy used it as their symbol in the fourteenth century. From then on it was recognised all over Europe as the pawnbroker's sign.

Well-made hanging signs composed of metal were once a familiar sight around Dublin, but have gradually been replaced by plastic signs, which are lighter and more cheaply made. The introduction of neon signs, some of which were very artistic, also contributed to the decline of the sign-maker's trade. One of the most elegant of the hanging signs in Dublin is the one at Greene's Bookshop in Clare Street, whose generous swan-neck curl is ornamented by fine leaves, scrolls and latticework.

Craftsmen also produced ironwork items for interior use, such as decorative grilles to protect windows, or ornate balustrades for stone staircases, as at Ely House or the Rotunda Hospital. In the interiors of houses and other buildings there is also an impressive array of dog-grates, stoves and fireplaces, mostly from the Victorian period.

It was in the late eighteenth century that cast iron really came into its own, and by the early nineteenth century there was widespread availability at reasonable cost and it was being used to mass-produce such items as railings. Household inventories that predate the Industrial Revolution reveal just how expensive all metal objects were. Everything, including nails, locks, hinges, bolts and gates, had to be handmade. It can be said, therefore, that iron was the pioneering material of the Industrial Revolution and one which the Victorians exploited to the full, making use of new technology to mass-produce cast-iron architectural features, such as rainwater goods (gutters and pipes), staircase details, window and floor gratings, security grilles, porches, pillars, fountains, lamps and many smaller items, such as door furniture (knockers, letterboxes, bell pulls), firegrates and stoves, plumbing and sanitary ware, balconies, finials and wall plaques. Many beautiful iron panels were mass-produced for garden gates, as gratings for heating systems and a host of other uses, giving rise to a wide variety of designs.

Cast iron was also used as early as 1816 in the construction of Dublin's famous Halfpenny Bridge, where its lightness and delicacy, combined with strength and ability to withstand rust, has stood the test of time. The fact that the metalwork of the bridge was fully restored for the first time in 2001 speaks for itself. Immense cast-iron piers and brackets support the bridges of the Loopline Railway, but the best examples are at Butt Bridge, where it spans the River Liffey.

Opposite page
Top: A wrought-iron lamp standard at Montpelier Parade, Monkstown, County Dublin. This elegant piece was made around 1800, with a crossbar to provide support for a lamplighter's ladder. The circular holder once held a glass globe in which an oil lamp burned.
Bottom: O'Connell Bridge boasts fine examples of three-branch cast-iron gas lights.

This page
Top: The beautiful Victoria fountain in Dun Laoghaire, with its domed top, was erected to commemorate Queen Victoria's last visit to Ireland in 1900. Decorated with birds, griffons, foliage, scrollwork and a bust of the Queen, it was manufactured by the McFarlane factory in Scotland, but was destroyed in 1981. A replica will be erected.
Above: The lion-mask knocker, with its bold and generous proportions, is typical of Victorian door furniture.
Left: A section of the balustrade of the King's Bridge, at Heuston Station. This beautiful cast-iron structure was erected in 1821.

Dublin Iron Founders

There were many iron foundries and iron merchants in eighteenth- and nineteenth-century Dublin. Among the most notable of them were the Phoenix Ironworks on Parkgate Street, Sheridan's Eagle Foundry on Church Street, Turner's Hammersmith works in Ballsbridge and the South City Foundry on Bishop Street. The South City Foundry was owned by Tonge and Taggart in the later nineteenth century and specialised in articles of street furniture, such as coal plates, drains and shores. The name is often seen on the streets of the city. There were several iron foundries located in the Church Street area, which were working even until recent times, and the still-thriving Hammond Lane Company originated there in a narrow street of that name.

Since the eighteenth century there has been a large number of ironmongers to be found in Dublin, especially in Capel Street. While iron founders made the artefacts, the ironmonger was there to sell them. Sometimes ironmongers had their own foundry, too. These firms sold a wide range of products, many of which bore their names on neat cast-iron plaques. Hodges & Sons of Westmoreland Street, Maguire and Gatchell of Dawson Street, Henshaw of Christchurch Place, Edmundson of Capel Street and Loftus Bryan of Bride Street were once very well-known names, and can still be seen on kitchen ranges, manhole covers, gates and railings. Kennan's of Fishamble Street was a noted manufacturer of gates and a wide variety of other artefacts. Ross and Walpole of 63-67 North Wall Quay, and Mallet and Spence were other notable firms who manufactured all manner of goods, including ships, bridges and heavy machinery. Mallet was the maker of the most striking Trinity College railings, those which front Nassau Street, and his name is embossed on them.

The name of Turner has been associated with the craft of ironwork in Dublin since the seventeenth century. For instance, the records of Trinity College show that the beautiful wrought-iron balustrade of the staircase in the Dining Hall was made in 1765 by Timothy Turner. He also supplied ironwork for the Provost's House and Regent House, the building that incorporates the front entrance to the college, and is

Opposite page

Top: The main entrance to Áras an Uachtaráin leads through a pair of magnificent, tall wrought-iron gates. They are composed of upright bars topped by ornamental scrollwork. The two circular discs are an unusual feature of such gates. Note the pair of gas lamps which surmount the gate piers. All such gates were designed with security in mind, and could be locked from either side.

Bottom: Detail of a Victorian garden gate from The Priory, Stillorgan. The metalwork, cleaned of paint, reveals the blacksmith's skill in shaping the material, and shows the rivets which join each piece to the main frame.

This page

Left: Airpark House, Rathfarnham, is fronted by a classic pair of plain Georgian entrance gates, which illustrate the strength of a simple design. The graceful drop, or curve in the top rail of the gates makes them less forbidding, while the standard double row of bars in the lower part of the gate was designed to keep small animals in or out. (Airpark was an attractive eighteenth-century house, of medium size, which was demolished to make way for the M50.)

Below: A mighty emblem of military prowess, this cast-iron suit of armour is one of a pair that sit atop the piers of the entrance gates to the Royal Hospital, Kilmainham. The symbolism is appropriate, given that the hospital was built to accommodate wounded soldiers.

recorded as the maker of the fine grille that has stood over the entrance gates to the Provost's House in Grafton Street since 1764.

To the side of the main entrance to the college lies a magnificent staircase of cantilevered stone and wrought iron, recorded in 1761 as comprising '59 panells of neat scrold work'. These scrollwork panels were made from flat bars of iron, less than one-quarter-of-an-inch thick (6.35mm) and about half-an-inch (12.7mm) in depth. Each handmade piece was modelled on a full-size template or design drawn on paper. The scrolls were forged from one length of iron and were held together with a collar and rivets. Similar ironwork dating from the mid-eighteenth century was made for the staircase and chapel gallery of the Rotunda Hospital. The hospital records show that this work was carried out by William Hutchins in 1758. Hutchins was paid £42 3s 2d for the staircase balustrade and £79 4s 0d for the gallery.

Ironmongers or blacksmiths, such as Turner and Hutchins, made their bread and butter by manufacturing commonplace objects, such as nails, screws, bolts, rivets and other important and necessary fittings. Timothy's descendant, Richard Turner, carried on the family business. The entrance gates to Dublin Castle at Palace Street and the gates to Tyrone House in Marlborough Street are stamped with his name.

In the 1870s there were three members of the Sheridan family involved with ironworks and bronze-casting in the city. The Sheridans and the Murphys (also of

Church Street) were noted for their casting of bronze bells for churches, farmyards and ships.

The firm of J&C M'Gloughlin, of Pearse Street, was founded in 1875 and was responsible for much of the highly decorative ironwork in Dublin's late Victorian buildings, including the gates and lamps at the Ulster Bank on College Green and a wide variety of church railings. For instance, the fine gates and railings of St Audoen's Church on High Street were made by them. In the twentieth century, M'Gloughlin's manufactured the large pair of gates for the Kildare Street entrance to Leinster House.

The construction of elaborate glasshouses and conservatories gave further scope for the art of the iron master. The Great Palm House, which is the largest glasshouse in the Botanic Gardens in Glasnevin, was erected in 1884. It was made in pre-cast sections by Boyd's of Paisley in Scotland and is an outstanding example of international importance. Nearby and somewhat older is the now restored curvilinear range, a long glasshouse structure designed and manufactured in Dublin by Richard Turner. It was begun in 1843, and forms the architectural centrepiece of the gardens. The structural

quality, decorative detail and refinement of Turner's work at Glasnevin places his foundry at the forefront of Irish ironwork.

While the eighteenth and nineteenth centuries marked the heyday of cast-iron usage, by the twentieth century it had become unfashionable and unwanted by designers. For instance, as railings in front of houses vanished, concrete walls were used in their place. Tiled hearths replaced the cast-iron fireplace and new forms of heating and cooking did away with articles such as ranges altogether.

Gates

The demand for gates peaked in the Victorian period with the construction of so many new suburban houses, all requiring gates. These included double gates for carriage entrances on large houses and single gates for pedestrian entrances to terraced houses. In Georgian

Above: The magnificent railings of Trinity College, which rise to a height of some fifteen feet (4.5m), including their granite plinth or wall, were cast at the Dublin foundry of Mallet. The spiked railings, which date from the second half of the nineteenth century, are supported by ironwork pilasters that bear the crest of Trinity College.

Below: Ironwork became a useful medium through which to symbolise the activity that was associated with a particular building. This simple gilt cross is part of the railings of the Pro-Cathedral in Marlborough Street, and dates from the completion of the church in 1830.

Opposite page

Top left: Cast-iron railings continued to be fashionable architectural accessories right up until the First World War and beyond. In this example from the late nineteenth century, the railing is composed of a series of decorative panels rather than the simpler bars or poles of early Victorian and Georgian styles. A great variety exists around the inner suburbs of Dublin, for example, in Donnybrook and Drumcondra. Such railings were generally painted black in urban areas with white preferred for coastal and country areas.

Top right: Examples of the Art Nouveau style are rare in Ireland, and very tame when compared to the extravagant flourishes that may be seen in Belgium or Eastern Europe. A hint of Art Nouveau is evident here in the railings of the Iveagh Buildings, built in 1904.

Below right: A typical cast-iron upright for the railings of Belgrave Square, Monkstown, dating from about 1860.

Below left: The railings for the Mansion House in Dawson Street were specially designed to incorporate the Dublin City coat of arms.

terraced houses, where a flight of steps led directly to the front door, gates were used for access to the basement area only and were discreetly fitted into the railings.

Many banks, shops and other business premises, such as the AIB on Dame Street, had attractive protective outer gates as a security measure. Such gates obviously needed to be secure, and most Georgian and Victorian gates are fitted with locks, though they are seldom still in use. An exception is the massive pair in Foster Place, which give access to the yard of the Bank of Ireland.

As demand increased, so too did the variety available. A manufacturer of gates had to be versatile and be able to turn his hand to ecclesiastical work, shop gates and grilles, handrails, enclosures for tombs, turnstiles, spiral staircases, fences and balustrades. Though there was a great deal of repetition in ironwork designs, there was also much scope for originality. One unique design is the wonderful composition of arrows which forms the gates to the Jesuit College at Milltown Park, in Milltown.

Many gates, especially those which once formed the entrance to a country house or farm, had an extra row of short bars in the lower section to prevent dogs and small animals from getting through. In the Georgian period, when wrought-iron gates tended towards simplicity, the top rail was usually dipped in the centre, though sometimes the opposite was the case, as in the beautiful example at Áras an Uachtaráin in the Phoenix Park. While these typical Georgian gates might make the entranceway extremely attractive, they also fulfil their other function of security, as is evident in the closeness of the upright bars and the presence of spikes on top. With the ready availability of cast-iron ornament in the Victorian period, gate designs became more and more elaborate. For example, the now-disused entrance gates to St Luke's Hospital, on Orwell Park, contain a decorative monogram and are surmounted by a pair of elaborate leaf scrolls.

Railings

The manufacture of railings for houses, churches and other buildings has always been one of the principal tasks

of the ironworker. Plain, square profile bars stood between the footpath and the houses of the Georgian terraces, while various, more elaborate patterns were utilised by the Victorians. For example, the railings at Christ Church Cathedral, erected in the 1870s, provided security for its immediate precinct and sport shamrock finials, while those protecting the Cork Hill entrance to Dublin Castle are appropriately decorated with axes.

While house railings could range from the very simple to the quite elaborate, those of public buildings, banks and churches tended to be of a larger scale and were heavier and more richly decorated. The gates and railings of Charleston Road Methodist Church (now converted to offices) are supported by massive cast-iron piers or pillars. Often such pillars supported a pair of gas or oil lamps.

Most railings are fixed to the stone coping of a low wall by means of a socket filled with molten lead. They were usually assembled in six- or nine-feet (1.8m or 2.7m) lengths or panels, which were riveted together. Cast-iron pillars or corner posts were also necessary to stabilise the railings, and one or more iron stays were needed to keep it rigid. Decorative spikes or railing heads were used both to ornament the railing and to make it difficult to climb.

Though railings comprised of upright bars continued to be the most common type used in the nineteenth century, decorative panels filled with scrolls and other designs were widely employed in late Victorian streets, such as Eglinton Road in Donnybrook. Railings were also used at this time for the new promenades in Bray and Dun Laoghaire, where they were generally painted in marine colours.

Church Ironwork

The Gothic revival that took place in the mid-nineteenth century is visible in many aspects of Dublin's architecture and in all of the arts and crafts associated with it. As the domination of classical taste dwindled, church architecture was reinvented through the adoption of the medieval styles of Romanesque and Gothic. The first, somewhat tame efforts consisted of a hybrid of Georgian and Gothic and date from the early 1800s. Examples of this style include St Michan's Catholic Church on Green Street, and the former SS Michael and John's Church on Blind Quay.

The later Victorian period saw the emergence of architects with a more purist historical approach, such as George Edmund Street, the

Above: Dun Laoghaire: this collection of railing heads, dating from 1830 to 1860, comes from the Dun Laoghaire area and is a sample of the forty or fifty variations which may be found. The African spearhead (*extreme left*) was used on railings and gates at Sydenham Terrace in Corrig Avenue, built *c.*1855. The *fleur-de-lis* (painted blue) comes from Gresham Terrace, erected in about 1830.

Right: A classic example from Merrion Square of the square-bar Georgian railing with corner post, which once supported a lamp.

Opposite page

Top: The decorative railings at Christ Church Cathedral with their shamrock finials.

Bottom right: The spiky Gothic style of these Victorian railings was much used in Victorian times for the perimeter of church precincts. This example was made by J&C M'Gloughlin.

architect who designed and oversaw the changes to Christ Church Cathedral carried out in the late nineteenth century. Street returned to the medieval use of stone – limestone for walls, with yellow sandstone for the mouldings of the Gothic windows. The move towards an almost archaeological accuracy in the Gothic style was given impetus by the writings of John Ruskin and Augustus Welby Pugin, which advocated the careful study and reproduction of original medieval features. The end result was Victorian Gothic churches that often replicated exactly the style and detail of fourteenth- and fifteenth-century churches of the kind found in England and Europe.

For these architects no detail was too small or insignificant, and when it came to ironwork grilles, hinges, locks and handles, great efforts were made to accurately copy earlier, richly elaborate examples. The doors of Victorian Gothic churches provided plenty of scope for making decorative hinges, as evidenced by the west doors, transept door and Chapter House door in Christ Church Cathedral. This marvellous ironwork dates from the mid-1870s. The massive ornate hinges that cover the doors of such buildings were originally designed as much to strengthen the wood as for decoration. A magnificent early example may be seen on the main entrance to Dr Steevens's Hospital, which was built during the 1720s. A highly ornate wrought-iron screen, completed in 1898, closes off the Lady Chapel from the main body of SS Augustine and John's Church at St John's Lane. The Gothic ironwork was painted red and gold and echoes the richly decorated interiors which Pugin and Ruskin so admired. The church was designed by Pugin's son, Edward, along with the associated firm of Ashlin and Coleman.

Balconies

Many Dublin houses of the late Georgian period are decorated with balconies. Considering that ironwork of this sort can be quite fragile and prone to neglect, a great number and variety of examples still exist. These highly decorative features gave emphasis to the first-floor windows, which was where they were usually placed. Single balconies, sometimes called balconettes, were large enough to stand out onto in order to take the air on a summer's afternoon, or to watch the world going by. But they were designed to be secure enough to prevent a child from falling out onto the pavement below, and to allow the tall, elegant windows, which in the late Georgian period often reached down to the floor, to be left open for ventilation.

The balcony was therefore an appendage of the late eighteenth-century Continental fashion for tall windows, which is why they were so plentiful in areas like Merrion Square, Leeson Street and North Great George's Street. They continued to be very popular until the mid-nineteenth century, and examples abound in districts such as Rathmines, where there are many houses dating from between 1830 and 1850. Some of the grander terraced houses, especially those of Merrion Square and Leeson Street, have full-width balconies that

span the three front windows of the façade, and these also remained popular until well into the nineteenth century.

The majority of balconies found in Dublin were assembled from front and side panels made from cast iron. The corner posts, flat handrail and heavy iron floor were usually made of wrought iron and were keyed into the masonry of the wall beside the window. It is a tribute to the quality of iron used that most of these are still in good condition, except where they have been completely neglected and have rusted away.

Balconies and window guards continued to be used in the Victorian period and many elaborate designs were available. The most common patterns included the honeysuckle motif, a lattice design with rosettes and a simple 'Gothic' design (c.1830) that incorporated two bands of quatrefoils. There were other combinations, mostly based on stylised foliage and medallions with ornamental posts. The average balcony was between thirty-three inches and thirty-five inches high (85cm and 90cm), but in some suburban and country areas they were kept low so as not to restrict a view.

This page

Above: An unusual hybrid porch and balcony, supported by Gothic-style cast-iron pillars. The decorative panels of this balcony comprise a favourite pattern of the early 1800s, and there are several examples of it in the Rathmines area.

Left: This section of cast-iron balcony once ornamented the porch of St Grellan's, an early Victorian house in Monkstown.

Opposite page

Top left: A late Georgian cast-iron balcony in the lattice style decorates a window in Leeson Street.

Bottom: A magnificent Victorian full-width balcony from a house on Merrion Square.

Verandas and Porches

The decorative ironwork that was available for balconies in the late eighteenth and early nineteenth centuries was also adapted for elaborate porches and verandas. In most cases these beautiful structures were added to buildings as an afterthought, or as part of a later addition to the main house. In several detached houses the addition of a ballroom, especially at first-floor level, provided an opportunity to erect a veranda, which was essentially a large balcony with a covering or roof above. A very fine example exists at Booterstown House, where it decorated the bow-shaped first-floor ballroom and allowed it to be fully ventilated without danger to the dancing guests.

By far the most elaborate example is the dramatic veranda that spans the whole garden front of Roebuck House. Its delicate white-painted tracery is beautifully contrasted against the mellow pink

brickwork behind. Access to the garden is provided by a graceful flight of iron steps, which widen as they descend. It is tempting to think that this ironwork may have been produced locally in Jackson's Ironworks, which was operating in the early 1800s at Clonskeagh Bridge.

A beautiful porch of similar design forms part of the garden front of Beechpark, Castleknock (*see* illustration, p.19). The delicate iron pilasters of scrollwork support a curved roof filled with coloured glass. The majority of this ironwork dates from the early decades of the nineteenth century, though further research is needed to ascertain the exact date and place of manufacture.

A most original porch at Gledswood, Clonskeagh, probably dating to about 1840, is composed of four Ionic-style pilasters containing diagonal bars and is semicircular in shape. This porch is deceptive, as it appears to be made of iron but is in fact constructed of timber. It is, however, very similar to various contemporary examples in iron. It may have been part of the original design for the house as it fits neatly into a recessed entrance bay and sits on a short flight of semicircular steps.

Staircases and Balustrades

In the eighteenth century wrought iron was generally used for the balustrades of stone staircases in very grand houses, such as Leinster House, 9 Henrietta Street and the Provost's House in Trinity College. By contrast, the staircases of public buildings tended to be less prominent and thereby less showy. Staircases designs ranged from simple upright bars with scroll details at the top and bottom to highly elaborate balusters with cast ornamentations. An example of the latter is the main staircase in Ely House, where the balustrade incorporates various animals, including a boar and a lion, while the rest of the ironwork is made up of ornate finials and medallions. The specially commissioned iron staircase at Belvedere College, Great Denmark Street (*c.*1785), features rectangular balusters ornamented with a cherub's head contained within a sunburst, a motif repeated elsewhere in the plasterwork of the house.

Such elaborate wrought iron was the exception rather than the rule, as most eighteenth-century and early nineteenth-century houses in Dublin had timber staircases and balustrades. It was not until the mid-nineteenth century that iron again became popular for staircases, but it was now mostly cast iron that was used. Fine Victorian houses in County Dublin, such as Leopardstown Park in Sandyford (1830s), The Slopes in Monkstown (1860s), or Glenageary House near Dun Laoghaire (1840s), had elaborate cast-iron staircase balustrades, some added during a later remodelling. Some time after 1877

Leopardstown Park, for example, was remodelled by James Talbot Power, the wealthy owner of Power's Distillery in Thomas Street. The house – later donated by his widow for use as a hospital, a purpose it still serves – is a fine example of the Italianate style. The bifurcated staircase with its solid cast-iron balustrade of spirals and miniature capitals is typical of the 1880s.

Monkstown House is an even more elaborate Italianate mansion, boasting a tall, cut-stone tower. It has a spacious hall and a stone staircase, on which the cast-iron balustrade is in the form of a continuous vine scroll.

Glenageary House was probably enlarged to the designs of JS Mulvany in the middle of the nineteenth century. The staircase ironwork, like that of The Slopes, was stamped with a Victorian registration mark, giving its date and place of manufacture. These ornate, somewhat Jacobean-style iron balusters decorated the main staircase, which became a spiral

in order to reach a rooftop belvedere or viewing tower.

There is a more classical or Georgian quality to the balustrades at Montebello in Killiney, which is a mid-Victorian house. Though cast-iron detail could be chosen from an iron foundry's catalogue and was less expensive than a wrought-iron equivalent, the latter is still sometimes found in Victorian buildings. The staircase at Farmleigh, Castleknock, made in the late nineteenth century, is a good example. Delicate wrought-iron panels of scrollwork and *repoussé* flowers make an attractive feature of the first- and second-floor landings.

Cast-iron spiral staircases were also available from catalogues, or could be made to order. A particularly tall spiral stairs in Dun Laoghaire Town Hall was erected in 1880 to provide access to a public clock and belfry. The Old Library in Trinity College, re-roofed about 1860, was also fitted with a fine cast-iron spiral staircase.

Above: The graceful scroll of this cast-iron staircase, with its leaf-and-tendril decorations, dates from 1859.
Left: This decorative balustrade was part of the original parapet of the Ballast Office at O'Connell Bridge, built in 1820.
Opposite page: Deansgrange House, built in the 1850s, has a sweeping, curved staircase with stylish cast-iron balustrade with a mahogany handrail.

Gutters

Gutters and rainwater pipes are for the most part fairly plain, but during the nineteenth and early twentieth century a wide range of designs became available from foundries and suppliers, such as Baxendale's, which had a large shop on Capel Street. Ornamental gutter brackets and a variety of gutter mouldings and hoppers (or rainwater heads), could be bought or ordered.

Box-shaped hoppers, such as those found on Christ Church Cathedral, and other Gothic designs are still to be seen around Dublin, but the most common type is the five-sided cast-iron model, which can be seen on almost any Victorian house.

Specially designed castings with rosettes, monograms or dates were available, as at Christ Church Cathedral, or Glenmaroon in Chapelizod where the hoppers bear the date 1904 – the year in which the house was completed. Though the most common downpipe was circular in shape, square and rectangular pipes were also manufactured and are often seen on Victorian public buildings, such as banks and churches. Sometimes the joints of gutters were disguised by an ornamental lion mask or other feature, as for instance at The Slopes, a now-vanished Victorian house in Monkstown.

Opposite page, top: A rectangular rainwater hopper on Christ Church Cathedral, dated 1875, records the year that George Edmund Street's work on the cathedral was completed.

Opposite page, middle: Newman House, St Stephen's Green: during the nineteenth century cast-iron gutters, pipes and hoppers replaced the lead rainwater goods which had been commonplace in the eighteenth century. This surviving lead hopper, dated 1766 and located at the rear of Newman House, is a rare feature.

Opposite page, bottom: Pipes were fixed to the wall by means of holdfasts or straps, of which there was a great variety.

This page, top: The dramatic gasholder at Ringsend was a major work of cast-iron manufacture. Note the pointed finials which ornament this utilitarian structure.

This page, above: A cast-iron hopper from a mid-Victorian business premises at the top of Eustace Street is embossed with Gothic detail.

This page, right: The cast-iron columns of the railway bridge at Westland Row are boldly ornamented with a studded and latticed pattern.

Firegrates

Today many people light fires in their homes as a secondary source of heat or, more often, simply because they like an open fire, but they rely on oil- or gas-fired central heating as their primary heat source. In the past, however, the open hearth was a focal point for the family, providing the only heat in the house. In what have become known as 'period houses' (any house built before 1930), one expects to find at least one good fireplace. Most will be made of cast iron, and many will have a marble or timber surround.

The iron firegrate is a relatively modern invention and was a product of the Industrial Revolution. Before the widespread availability of coal, people mainly burned timber in their fireplaces and made use of cast-iron firebacks to throw out heat. A fireback is a solid plate of iron, usually cast with some decorative device on one side, such as a coat of arms. Few examples survive in Dublin, but there is one fireback from an eighteenth-century house on Arran Quay, which can be seen in the National Museum. Coal-burning firegrates began to be mass-produced in the late eighteenth century, and it was the norm to find them in Dublin's Georgian houses. The abolition of the coal tax in 1793 greatly encouraged the use and manufacture of such cast-iron grates.

In the nineteenth century house designs changed to include a greater number of smaller-sized rooms in response to the demand for greater comfort and warmth. As a result, more firegrates were required. This increase in demand coincided with the increased availability of coal in Britain, which was also imported into Ireland in very large quantities. A significant number of successful coal merchants established themselves in Dublin during the Victorian period and in large part owed their prosperity to the humble firegrate.

Two magnificent examples were discovered during the demolition of 29 Clare Street. These grates date from *c.*1760 to 1780 and were made by the Carron Company, a noted iron foundry in Falkirk, Scotland, in which the famous architects and designers Robert and John Adam had a commercial interest. The uprights of the grate are ornamented with urns in high relief. (An interesting cast-iron bread oven, also by Carrons, which was made for the Cabinet Office in 10 Downing Street, is on display in the Museum of London.)

The influence of the Adam brothers on late eighteenth-century design and decoration cannot be underestimated. The term 'Adam style' is synonymous with delicate and tasteful Georgian architecture and ornament, and its pervasive influence spread beyond England and Ireland to America. In 1775 Robert and James Adam published *Works in Architecture*, a self-advertising record of their prolific output and of their magnificent house designs in the elegant classical style. Robert Adam, the master hand, evolved his own decorative style, copied and developed from original classical sources. The book contained his beautiful designs for buildings and their decorative detail, including stonework, plasterwork, joinery and ironwork.

Other designers and makers, such as William Glossop, produced illustrations of firegrates in books such as *The Stove Maker's Assistant*, published in 1771. These show cast- and wrought-iron grates, often with a curved basket, lifted about twelve inches (30cm) off the floor and supported at the front by ornate legs. The grates were further ornamented by brass fretwork, urns and a tooled or decorated brass fire surround. This was typical of a high-quality, handmade eighteenth-century grate, examples of which can be found in the principal reception rooms of many Dublin houses of the Georgian period. The new cast-iron grates were also used, but would have been

considered less showy. Many old cast-iron grates survive in bedrooms, where fireplaces were less often interfered with, modernised, or removed.

The most common early cast-iron grate in Dublin was the hob grate, which contained a small fire basket with an ornamental fireback and two decorated uprights. These grates, designed for burning coal, ranged in size from fourteen inches to thirty-six inches (35.5cm–91.4cm) in width, and were built into the brickwork of the chimney. The very smallest grates were designed for top-floor bedrooms.

Register grates became popular in the early nineteenth century and were designed with a closed back and sides with a small, adjustable opening to the chimney. This meant that the draught of the fire could be controlled, thereby saving coal and preventing the fire from smoking. The fronts of these register grates were often ornamented with florid acanthus leaves and other motifs.

By about 1850 the arched-plate register grate had become commonplace and was the sort most frequently seen in a good Victorian fireplace. The whole grate, made of separate pieces of cast iron bolted together, was usually square in order to fit into the brick opening of the chimney and the surround of the marble chimney piece. The opening was arched with sides curving in to meet the grate, which was fronted by two or three bars. Varying degrees of ornamentation were applied to the arch, from simple rope mouldings to over-elaborate patterns of scrolls, vines and beads. Further advances on the design of grates took place in the late nineteenth century, including the use of firebricks and a closed front that incorporated an ash pan.

By about 1880 new designs started to utilise tiled panels on either side of the grate, and more costly marble or timber surrounds began to be replaced so that the whole fireplace was now made of cast iron. The new tiled grates were rectangular in shape and were usually fitted with a decorated hood or canopy, which could be adjusted. The hoods were mostly made of cast iron, but the early 1900s saw the appearance of copper hoods bearing florid Art Nouveau designs.

Previous pages

Page 40 and 41: On either side are the side panels, or cheeks, of an eighteenth-century hob grate from 29 Clare Street, a house which has now vanished. The grate was made by Carron of Falkirk to a very bold design.

Page 40, bottom: These two late Georgian basket or hob grates are examples of the widely varying styles that were available.

Page 41, top: The Victorian arched firegrate, which was lined with tiles, became the standard shape for grates in the nineteenth century.

Opposite page

Above left: A rectangular front from a mid-nineteenth-century firegrate.

Below left: An early nineteenth-century doorknocker, in the form of a hand, also once quite commonplace on the doors of the city.

This page

Top and bottom right: Fine examples of Victorian brass letter boxes.

Middle: A brass lion-mask knocker from a house in North Great George's Street. A stunning example of the detailed casting that was available in the Georgian period.

Bottom middle: An early example of a cast-iron knocker from the Georgian period, a type commonly associated with Dublin's doors. The female head is a very typical design and has been much reproduced.

Coal Plates

A fascinating variety of circular iron plates, known in Dublin as coal-hole covers, ornament many of the older pavements in front of the city's Georgian terraces. Their purpose was to provide access to the cellars with which all Georgian and Victorian houses were equipped, and which were located either under the steps leading to the front door, or under the footpath in front of the house. The coal plates covered a circular hole that was cut into the stone slab of the pavement, which enabled a delivery of coal, turf, or logs to be made by simply tipping the fuel into the cellar beneath. These artefacts of street furniture were first used in the mid-eighteenth century when the consumption of coal increased markedly, and they continued to be manufactured until the end of the nineteenth century.

Coal plates were generally twelve inches (30cm) in diameter, but some were as wide as fourteen inches (35.5cm), and were usually about half-an-inch (12.7mm) thick. Most had a ring cast into the underside of the plate, and this was affixed to the cellar wall by means of a chain. The purpose of the chain was to secure it to the inside wall and thus prevent thieves from breaking into the house by sending a child in through the cellar!

A householder could expect to pay between 2/6 and 5/- for a coal plate in the early nineteenth century. They were cast in moulds

— usually made of sand — into which a carved wooden design or template was pressed. The designs used to ornament the coal-hole covers were inspired by mathematical and natural patterns, which were eminently appropriate to their form and function. These included exploding stars, patterns of leaves and petals and other abstract motifs, all usually encircled by a beaded rim. The oak leaf was also a popular design. Some late nineteenth-century examples also bore the maker's name, such as that of the South City Foundry at Bishop Street. Dublin's coal-hole covers have survived remarkably well, apart from the wearing and polishing of their patterns by the centuries of passing pedestrians.

Lamps

This page

Top: The most unusual lamps of Neary's pub in Chatham Street are held aloft by a most realistically modelled truncated arm. These are typical of the late nineteenth century. Hands were often featured as hinges for gates, an example of which can be seen on the entrance gates to the National Concert Hall, or were employed in door-knocker design, an example of which can be seen on p.42.

Opposite page

Top right: This Gothic-style bracket, to be found at the Chapel Royal in Dublin Castle, reflects the design of the chapel itself. It was originally designed as an oil lamp, but is now electrified.

Middle right: At College Green four elegant gas lamp standards, ornamented by wonderful seahorses, once surrounded the statue of Henry Grattan. The lamps, only two of which now remain, date from the mid-nineteenth century and are still in use and bear the Corporation's coat of arms on each side of their triangular bases.

Bottom right: An early electric light of swan-neck design, the prototype of which was introduced in 1892 and was the first public electric street light in Dublin. Many variations, incorporating shamrock motifs, were subsequently produced for the streets of Dublin City. For example, modern replicas may be seen in Dawson Street.

Bottom left: Modern lamps that borrow traditional elements of design have been installed on the new walkway at Sir John Rogerson's Quay.

Dublin's street lighting makes an important contribution to the range of street furniture in the city and adds greatly to the variety of decorative ironwork that has survived. Examples of oil, gas and electric lights were well documented in Derry O'Connell's *The Antique Pavement*, which was published by An Taisce in 1975. A number of oil lamp holders or brackets may be seen around the city, and fine examples include those at the entrances to the Chapel and Exam Hall in Trinity College, about the Chapel Royal in Dublin Castle, and under the colonnade of the Bank of Ireland in College Green. These brackets were generally placed over doors or entrances in order to shed the maximum amount of light. They were never positioned very high, allowing the lamplighter to replenish the oil, clean the glass and trim the wick with ease. The iron brackets at the Corn Exchange on Burgh Quay, dating from 1820, are good examples, although the lamps are missing.

There were once many ornate wrought-iron lamp holders forming part of the railings around the city's Georgian streets and squares, but most of those have disappeared. Some were removed, but more simply rusted away due to neglect and want of painting. However, plain examples do survive at Montpelier Parade in Monkstown and on several of the older churches around the city.

Many of James Malton's famous prints of Dublin, made in the 1790s, show these oil lamps attached to buildings and railings, where they were positioned to light the pavements, street corners and bridges of the city. The light that came from them was poor in comparison with that from gas lights, which were first introduced to the city in 1825. This new form of power coincided with the increasing popularity of cast iron, and by the mid-nineteenth century a rich array of designs for gas lamp standards was in production. Although hidden away in odd corners of the city, in church grounds and on public buildings, a surprising variety remains to be discovered.

The Five Lamps, said to have been made in 1897 as a monument to General Henry Hall of the Indian Army, is probably one of the best known and most elaborate of the various lamps. It not only incorporates five lamps, which represent the junction of five streets, but also has a drinking fountain at its base.

In College Green there is a fine pair of lamp standards supported by seahorses and bearing the city arms, which also date from the late nineteenth century. They were once part of a group of four lamps that surrounded the statue of Henry Grattan. Other examples of this period include the lamps at the entrance to the Mansion House, the lamps on O'Connell Bridge (erected in 1881) and those at City Hall.

Even the mundane gas street lights of the mid-nineteenth century were beautifully proportioned, elegant pieces of design, usually sporting rounded, fluted bases, leaf mouldings, fluted shafts and a crossbar for the lamplighter's ladder. Good examples may be seen in the Phoenix Park, where gas light was restored in the 1980s.

The arrival of electric lighting to the streets of the capital in 1892 introduced a new style of cast-iron lamp standard. These were even taller, as they did not need to be maintained every day by a lamplighter, and the greater height resulted in increased light and better visibility. The tops of these new lamps gave rise to some interesting designs, including swan-neck pillars and straight poles with elaborate semicircular scrolls incorporating, appropriately, Irish shamrocks. These 'shamrock lamps' were popular in the early 1900s and were erected by various local authorities, such as the Rathmines and Rathgar Township. The design has been reproduced several times since.

Brick and Terracotta

Dublin is a city of bricks. Though the city's major public buildings were generally built of stone, the most memorable streets are lined with houses and buildings built of brick. The greater part of the city's historic domestic architecture was built of it in the eighteenth and nineteenth centuries, and the predominant colour of Dublin is that of brick: the orangey-grey Georgian terraces, the russet-faced houses of Merrion Square, and the reds of suburban streets in Glasnevin, Clontarf, Ringsend, or Terenure. Brick was already widely in use in the seventeenth century, but extant examples are very rare. The brick of the Georgian period was handmade and usually produced in local brickworks around the city, such as the large brickfields at Sandymount. Most of the bricks were russet or red in colour, but some, such as those from Dolphin's Barn and Clonsilla, were yellow. The warm red colour was produced by the iron content of the clay, while a yellow tint was due to the presence of magnesium.

A small proportion of the city's eighteenth-century brick is known from custom's records to have come into Dublin as ballast on ships, but its quality varied considerably. At that time bricks were fired in a clamp – a huge temporary oven or bonfire of bricks and firing material. The bricks placed at the centre of the clamp tended to have a purple hue because they were over-baked, while those on the outside remained yellowish or 'uncooked' and consequently were weaker. The very best bricks were retained for the façade of the proposed building, while inferior ones were used for filling

Opposite page: The fanciful Gothic architecture of the South City Markets in South Great George's Street dates from 1878. It is composed of brick and terracotta and is one of Dublin's largest Victorian buildings, with shops fronting on four streets and a large internal arcade.

cavities in walls, or for rough work that might not be seen. Tuck-pointing – a method of enhancing a brick façade by means of thin, lime mortar joints and a red dye applied to the brick – was popular in the eighteenth century. It was a way of disguising an inferior-quality brick. A brick-maker could mould, by hand, anything from 2,000 to 10,000 bricks per day, depending on his skill. He was assisted in this enterprise by two boys and a carrier.

In the nineteenth century bricks were machine-produced and fired in a kiln. One of the earliest machines for moulding and cutting bricks was made in St Petersburg in 1807. By the Victorian period, bricks were mass-produced using purer clays, wire-cutting machines and coal-burning, which guaranteed consistent temperatures. As a result, these new bricks were not only harder and more durable but were also perfect in form and colour, removing the accidental colours and textures and the subtle varieties of shape and hue that had been evident previously. These machine-made bricks were smooth-textured, usually with a glazed or shiny surface.

These advances in brick-making meant that a range of decorative elements began to find their way into the manufacturer's repertoire. Ornamental brick was produced to a limited extent in Ireland, especially in Belfast, but in the later nineteenth and early twentieth centuries many elaborate bricks and panels of terracotta, along with copings and finials, were imported from England and Wales, where they were mass-produced. These imported bricks supplemented the types of ornamental brick available in Ireland and satisfied the growing demand for special designs.

But that is not to say that Irish brick-makers were outdone in the field by their British counterparts. There was plenty of work

for domestic producers too, for example, a variety of special bricks and terracotta ornament was manufactured at the Annadale Works in Belfast's Ormeau Road, and in Arklow. Most of the Victorian brick manufacturers stamped the 'frog', or hollow side, of their bricks with the name of their works, leaving a record of the most prominent: Portmarnock, Mount Argus, Dolphin's Barn, Clonsilla, Boghall (Bray) and Kingstown (Pottery Road, Dun Laoghaire). So far, any lists or catalogues of ornate bricks from Irish brickworks have failed to come to light.

Many of the commercial premises in the city's main shopping districts, such as Grafton, Dawson, Westmoreland and Henry streets, were rebuilt in the late nineteenth or early twentieth centuries, and made extensive use of the new decorative features. The building for Drummond's Seeds on Dawson Street, built in 1903, is a fine example, while major department stores, such as Todd Burns (now Penney's) on Mary Street and Arnott's on Henry Street, were also faced in brick and terracotta.

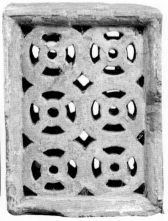
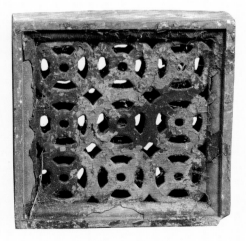

Most of the shops on George's Street Upper and George's Street Lower in Dun Laoghaire and on Main Street, Blackrock, were rebuilt in red brick between 1895 and 1910, often making use of highly decorative features. This rebuilding was a condition of the renewal of the ninety-nine-year lease and the landlord's architect appeared to have specified red brick for the upper floors of all new buildings.

Brick was considered appropriate for the building of bank branches and utilitarian structures, such as markets, baths and warehouses. The grand scale of the South City Markets at South Great George's Street is probably the city's most extravagant example of ornate brickwork and costly terracotta detail. The George's Street building, begun in 1878 to replace dilapidated markets, was designed in the Gothic idiom by the English

This page

Top: A small panel of flowers ornaments the brick wall of a house on Eglinton Road, Donnybrook.

Above: A striking lion mask from the centrepiece of an entrance gate to a private house on Merrion Road, opposite the RDS. This dramatic piece of terracotta probably dates from the 1890s.

Right: Beautiful long panels of terracotta ornament the Bank of Ireland at the corner of Parnell Square on Parnell Street, just opposite the Gate Theatre. The panels show a boldly modelled plant with flowers, perhaps a lily, rising from a tall classical urn.

Opposite page

Top: The Iveagh Trust Buildings were part of a large complex of housing, hostel and other educational buildings erected by the Earl of Iveagh at his own expense in the early 1900s.

Middle: In historical terms, one of Dublin's newest thoroughfares is Lord Edward Street, created in 1886 to connect Dame Street to Christ Church Place. At its corner with Fishamble Street is a fine brick and terracotta building, formerly The Boys' Home, now Kinlay House. A pair of griffons decorated the gable facing Christ Church Cathedral.

Bottom: This balustrade, entirely prefabricated in terracotta, was a standard staircase balustrade for houses or gardens, but was clearly made to order for this house on Eglinton Road, Donnybrook. Terracotta of this type was not cheap, but would have been far less costly than its equivalent in stone.

architects Lockwood and Mawson. The Camden Market, built in 1905 off Camden Street, is another typical example of the late Victorian fashion for this material.

Terracotta

Terracotta was widely used in the Middle East and Egypt in pre-Christian times and later by the Romans who employed it to make urns and statues and many other ornaments. Terracotta means 'burnt earth', and although the term is generally applied to decorative features, its process of manufacture is the same as that of brick. Clay is placed in a mould, then turned out, dried and finally fired in a kiln. The process demands great skill, especially for large ornamental objects. A degree of shrinkage must be allowed for and every detail has to be accurate. A very fine clay, or slip, was used for making terracotta so that no detail would be lost. The clay was treated or ground in a pug-mill until it was of sufficiently fine quality. The method of brick-making was the same as that employed in the manufacture of terracotta floor tiles, chimney pots, roof tiles, drains and garden ornaments. Most large pieces of terracotta, such as urns or fancy gables with finials or balls, would have been composed of several individual pieces which would then have been joined together to make the final product.

One of the earliest and most interesting forms of terracotta was the eighteenth-century manufacture of Coade stone. Coade stone was the invention of George and Eleanor Coade, who successfully made casts of a wide variety of sculptural and architectural objects using a secret recipe. Their method resulted in a very tough material. Among the few examples of Coade stone still on view in Dublin are the plaques and frieze which ornament the Rotunda on Parnell Square, at the top of O'Connell Street. Originally erected in 1764, the Rotunda was remodelled by James Gandon in 1786, at which time the decoration was added. This was at the height of the Coades's popularity and success. Elsewhere on Parnell Square, keystones featuring heads stamped with the Coade name may be seen on the arched cellars in the basement of 38 Parnell Square.

A Coade stone sphinx and lion stand guard on the surviving wing of Aldborough House, a late eighteenth-century mansion located at the Five Lamps. The elegant Rutland Fountain on Merrion Square, which stands in front of the National Gallery, is decorated with Coade stone medallions and figurative panels.

Terracotta was little used in Ireland before 1860. The catalogue of the Irish Industrial Exhibition of 1853 noted that terracotta, although popular in French and German cities, like Paris, Toulouse and

Above: Baggot Street Hospital, known originally as the Royal City of Dublin Hospital, is an imposing hospital building that makes magnificent use of yellow terracotta and red brick in an elaborate Flemish Renaissance style.

Opposite page, and this page, below: The Iveagh Baths was designed by English architects Joseph, Smithem and Joseph, and the building work was overseen by the Dublin firm of Kaye, Parry and Ross. This firm also planned the majority of the new shop premises in Dun Laoghaire's George's Street, mostly dating from the late 1890s and early 1900s. This example, bearing a date tablet '1898', has handsome window architraves, fluted pilasters and an arched parapet, all made in terracotta by the Ruabon Brickworks in West Wales, and shipped across the Irish Sea to Dun Laoghaire harbour.

Berlin, had not yet made any impact on Dublin:

> *'One of the great drawbacks under which Dublin and many other cities in these countries labour is the dull monotony of the unvaried walls of brick; with rectangular apertures for windows, and doors which seem to have been all made from the same design. The introduction of terracotta ornaments into the decoration of houses would banish this monotony and help to communicate life and picturesqueness to our cities.'*
> (Irish Industrial Exhibition catalogue, p.94. Published 1854.)

The contributor to the catalogue commented that though Ireland possessed an abundance of materials for the production of bricks, tiles and terracotta, there were few suitable clays exhibited and only five Irish brick manufacturers were represented at the exhibition. There was one Irish terracotta exhibitor, the rest coming from Scotland, England and Germany. The standard of production in those areas was very high, for example, the Farnley Iron Company, located near Leeds, exhibited a range of very elaborate vases and pedestals, urns, balusters, architectural mouldings and chimney pots.

The nature and source of this commentator's criticism was typical of the growing Victorian taste for ornament. The massive spread of Dublin's mid-Victorian suburbs was almost entirely constructed of red brick, and an inventiveness in the use of brick slowly evolved.

Above: Among the most unusual buildings in Dublin is the delightfully unorthodox Sunlight Chambers, which stands guard, overlooking the River Liffey, at the corner of Parliament Street and Essex Quay. It was designed as the Irish headquarters of Sunlight Soap, a large English-based company, and was completed in 1901. The English architect, Edward Ould, chose the Florentine palace as his model, and added two ceramic friezes to the façade, which adopt the style and colouring of Italian Renaissance examples. The images on the friezes represent the story of soap, its manufacture and use and the process of washing. At the time of its completion, it was fashionable to mock Sunlight Chambers for its exuberant use of ornament and colour, which some architectural critics saw as pretentious. Designed as an office building, the interior is by contrast very dull and plain. The friezes are adorned by lively coloured ceramics and are crowded with people engaged in ploughing, gathering olives, launching a boat and collecting water at a well and working at a medieval-type outdoor wash-house.
Opposite, bottom left: Several roundels incorporating languid female figures ornament the ground floor of the building.

Red, yellow and purple brick was used in a wide variety of ways, as string courses, arches and for fancy cornices. Chimney stacks, porches and front garden walls gave great scope for original brickwork with special ornamental bricks often used. Dog-tooth, chamfered and beaded bricks began to be included in designs, so that even the humblest dwelling could be enhanced.

Ceramic Pieces

The magnificent door surrounds in the National Museum were made in Italy in the style of the Renaissance designer Luca Della Robbia of Florence (*see* illustration, p.12). Their elaborate composition – in white, yellow and dark blue – is framed by pilasters ornamented with complicated arabesques. The overdoor is formed by a panel displaying an urn surrounded by cherubs, and a pair of brackets support a frieze and pediment above. The majolica, or ceramic work, was made at Burmantoft's in Leeds. These colourful features were once overpainted, but have since been impeccably cleaned and repaired by ceramic restorer Desirée Shortt.

56

Dublin's other great example of Victorian ceramic decoration is the pictorial frieze on the Sunlight Chambers at Essex Quay, which was completed in 1901, the year of Queen Victoria's death. The design of this extraordinary corner building, which was erected as the offices of Lever Brothers, the English soap manufacturers, was inspired by the architecture of Florentine palaces.

Pages 56-57, various discs: Among a small number of examples where ceramic art and terracotta have been used to good effect on modern buildings is the Setanta Centre on Nassau Street with its massive ceramic mural in the courtyard facing the Kilkenny Design shop. An interesting series of medallions was commissioned in the early 1990s from the Dublin-based firm of Cartin Ceramics for a group of houses which were erected on Bride Street by Dublin Corporation. Being close to the birthplace of Dean Jonathan Swift, it was decided that the subject matter should represent the stories of *Gulliver's Travels*.

Chimney Pots

Chimney pots represent another field of design and manufacture where ornamentation is used to good effect. A wide variety of pots can be seen on Dublin's houses. Most pots were produced in a yellow clay and were about two-and-a-half feet (1m) tall. The earliest known chimney pots, or cans, were a simple cylindrical shape with a moulded lip at the top. They were generally made by brick-makers or potters who produced rough earthenware for manufacturing and everyday use. One of the most commonplace and plainest varieties is the Dublin Pot, which is less than two-and-a-half feet (1m) in height and is slightly tapered towards the top with a moulded flange.

There was little variety in shape until the mid-nineteenth century. A typical pot of about 1830 was cylindrical with a moulded rim at the top and bottom. But the technical advances of the Victorian period resulted in a vast array of chimney-pot types. They were now available in octagonal and square shapes, as well as circular. The caps and bases were usually elaborately moulded in the form of cornices or crowns, and in some cases the tops were pierced with hearts or trefoil openings to improve the draught.

Unfortunately, few chimney pots bear the stamp of their maker, so it is difficult to establish with any degree of certainty where they were all made. However, the catalogue of the Irish Industrial Exhibition of 1853 illustrates some of the most ornate models made by the Farnley Iron Company in Leeds, and it is likely that most of the more elaborate examples were manufactured in England. Some of the late nineteenth-century dark-glazed models, such as the Champion Chimney Pot made by Peytons in England, were designed with louvred vents at the base in order to improve the draught of the chimney.

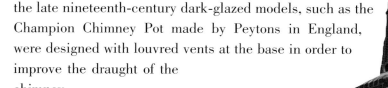

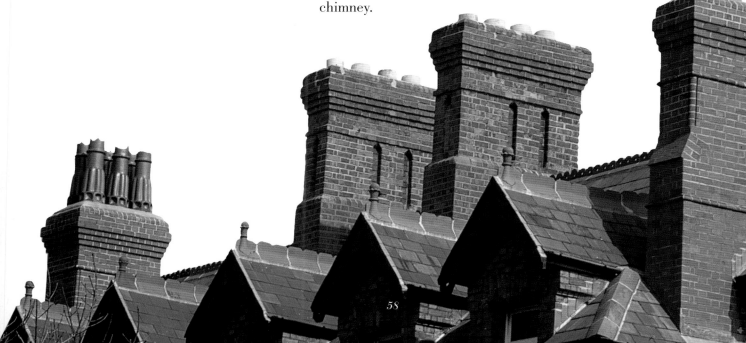

Opposite page

Top: A pair of tall Victorian chimney stacks, from a house on Monkstown Road, topped by a pair of typical Dublin 'cans'. This is the most common type of Victorian chimney pot to be found in Dublin.

Bottom: Harcourt Terrace displays elaborate brick chimney stacks, typical of the late nineteenth century. The pots at the extreme right and left are the special patented Champion design. It is important to remember that Victorian Dublin was a very smoky city as coal was the only form of fuel available.

This page

Above: Examples of three Victorian Dublin chimney pots.

Right: The smoke stack or chimney of the Turkish Baths in Bray, now vanished, had a somewhat oriental flavour.

Below: The tallest chimneys in Dublin are those of the ESB Generating Station at Poolbeg, which dominate Dublin Bay. The chimneys are over 600 feet (183m) in height and were constructed of concrete in the 1970s.

Windows

A building without windows would seem to contradict the basic human demand for natural light and the need to be able to see the outside world while being at a safe remove from it. Windows create the necessary balance between privacy and transparency, a balance that all-glass structures, like conservatories or some office buildings, do not have. Some public buildings, such as prisons, theatres and art galleries, were and are designed without windows in their outer wall for functional and sometimes security reasons, and also to reinforce the message that tells us what purpose the building serves. The type of window chosen and how it is used is, therefore, a key element in architectural design.

Since the origins of classical architecture, the window has provided unlimited scope for decorative design, in terms of shape, manner of articulation, type of moulding and architrave and choice of glazing. Prior to and during the seventeenth century windows were made to swing out. These casement-type windows, as they were called, are still commonplace in most European countries. In castles and important buildings, casements were usually fitted into stone mullions or frames, but the window frames in ordinary houses would have been made of timber, probably oak. We know from early

drawings that the glazing consisted of small diamond, or rectangular panes of glass held in position with lead. As we have already seen, however, no complete medieval buildings survive in Dublin with their decorative features and, apart from the Royal Hospital, Kilmainham, nothing from the seventeenth century remains either. (It should be noted that the original windows of the Royal Hospital were replaced during the eighteenth century.)

The strongest architectural legacy in Dublin, therefore, is that of the eighteenth century, from which many original windows are still in use and may be seen in their original context. The windows on the ground floor of Marsh's Library and those of the Old Library in Trinity College are early examples of the wooden sliding-sash window, which took root in England, Holland and Ireland in the late seventeenth and early eighteenth centuries and later found its way to North America, where it is very widespread today. The sliding-sash gradually replaced casement types with their small leaded windows, and the new larger panes of glass were popular because they admitted more light to the interiors of buildings.

The windows of the early eighteenth century had heavy glazing bars up to one-and-a-half

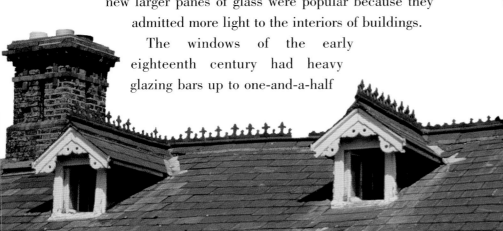

inches thick (3.8cm) and the window itself was an integral part of the overall design. The rectangular pattern of these typical Georgian sash windows harmonised with the architectural lines of classical architecture – a whole new style of building that was taking over from earlier structures. The white- or stone-coloured paint used on the wooden sashes accentuated the vertical emphasis of the window itself, while the horizontal glazing bars echoed the string courses and cornices and were matched internally by the arrangement of the shutters and panels. By the mid-eighteenth century sash windows were universal and could be seen everywhere from the grandest public buildings to the humblest cottages.

During the second half of the eighteenth century a great number of the older Dutch-gabled houses that lined the streets were cleared away and replaced by taller houses of more regular proportions. In Dublin, some of this work was carried out by the Wide Streets Commissioners, the body that dictated the scale and appearance of the new houses which lined the recently widened streets. The position of the windows in these new Georgian streetscapes was vital to the overall design, and despite later alterations many streets still retain their essentially Georgian character. Examples include parts of Dame Street, Parliament Street, Westmoreland Street and D'Olier Street.

The typical Georgian window is set back from the façade of the building by about five inches (12.7cm), allowing for the creation of a reveal – a plastered surround that is usually painted white. Internally these Georgian windows had timber architraves and were sometimes designed with elaborate bases of panelling and pedestals. The chunky classical mouldings were often lugged and shouldered at the top, in imitation of Palladian models. The joinery in the former St Ultan's Hospital in Charlemont Street is typical of the style (*see* illustration, p.113).

In the later eighteenth century, from 1770 onwards, it became the fashion to extend the windows of the main reception rooms on the first floor so that they reached almost from floor to ceiling. These were the grandest rooms in the house, situated on what was known as the *piano nobile*, or the noble floor, and were used for entertaining. Examples on Merrion Square, Mountjoy Square and North Great George's Street show that this arrangement flooded the rooms with light and looked extremely elegant. To stand inside such a room and look out onto the green and leafy squares below is part of the magic of Dublin's Georgian houses. The scale of these windows is impressive, sometimes reaching ten feet (3m), or twelve feet (3.5m) in height. Iron balconies were often added, partly as protection for when the lower sash was fully raised, and partly to provide access for further views of the street. As the eighteenth century progressed, the glazing bars

became thinner with more refined mouldings, resulting in delightfully delicate and graceful-looking windows.

The fact that so many beautiful timber windows have survived for more than 200 years, often in perfect condition, is a tribute to the well-seasoned wood that the joiners and carpenters used. There were many joinery workshops in Dublin where such windows could have been made, although craftsmen sometimes made and assembled their work on site.

Glass-blowers usually made bottles and other objects as well as window glass. Early glass, known as crown or spun glass, was hand-made and glass-blowers spun the spherical ball of hot molten glass until a wide disc was formed. Panes of glass were then cut from the circular sheet, leaving the bullion, or bullseye, in the middle as a sort of reject, considered fit only for the windows of an inn, or for the back basement of a house. A staircase window at the back of Dublin's oldest pub, The Brazen Head, contains several examples of this type of bullion glass. Old glass has a delicate rippled, or curved, irregular surface that can reflect light in unpredictable ways and slightly distort the view from inside. It has always been necessary to replace and repair windows as they are prone to get broken or disintegrate due to neglected maintenance. Many eighteenth-century windows, for example, in Merrion Square, were replaced in Victorian times with what was then new and fashionable: the larger panels of cylinder sheet glass and the flawless single panes of plate glass. Despite this,

the great majority of original eighteenth-century windows survived intact until recent times. During the last thirty years of the twentieth century, however, the aggressive marketing first of aluminium, then of uPVC windows has brought about the replacement of a huge number of old windows by inappropriate new models.

The production of glass and the glazing of windows was a reasonably profitable business in eighteenth-century Dublin. Contemporary maps and newspaper advertisements tell us that there were several glassworks, known as glasshouses, in the city – one at Mary's Lane, two on Abbey Street and another at Ringsend. The glasshouses were identified by their tall cone- or bottle-shaped kilns, which were notoriously smoky and could cause dangerous accidental fires. The Abbey Street Glassworks, which was near Marlborough Street and quite close to James Gandon's new Custom House, was described by a newspaper in 1793 as an 'abominable nuisance', spouting forth 'clouds of smoke that can only be likened to the discharges of thundering Etna.' Glasshouses were generally located within easy reach of the seashore from where one of the main ingredients, fine sand, could be readily obtained.

A glass and window tax that came into force in the early nineteenth century may have led to the closure of some Irish glasshouses, but there is no obvious evidence that windows in buildings became any less in number or smaller in scale. There may have been occasional instances of windows being blocked up in order to minimise the liability for window tax.

Besides the usual rectangular windows, which were common in the principal rooms of buildings, arched, round and sometimes oval windows were also made for staircases, attics and gable walls. Curved or quadrant windows were made for bow-shaped rooms, which were quite common at the back of Georgian houses. Grand Venetian windows, comprising an arched opening flanked by sidelights, were a favourite device in important mansions, such as Clanwilliam House on St Stephen's Green and Powerscourt Town House Centre on South William Street.

Wyatt windows became commonplace in the early 1800s and were also composed of three separate sections, which allowed ample light into a room. The Diocletian window, of which examples can be seen

Opposite page: This Georgian Gothic staircase window at Danesmote, Rathfarnham, dates from the late eighteenth century.

This page

Top: Malahide Castle, dating from the early nineteenth century. This window was inserted during modernisation of the castle and was chosen because its Gothic style was appropriate to the medieval character of the castle.

Bottom: Circular windows, such as this pretty example from Johnstown-Kennedy, were often found in passageways and back staircases. The house, which was demolished in the 1980s, dates to the mid-eighteenth century.

in the Chapel at Trinity College, or in the House of Lords (now the Bank of Ireland, College Green), was a further variation on this tripartite design. It originated in ancient Rome during the time of the emperor Diocletian.

Lantern windows, sometimes referred to as skylights, were used to light internal spaces, such as stairwells and passageways. They presented a particular challenge to the joiner and glazier alike. Lanterns were sometimes square, but circles and ovals were more usual. In the nineteenth century cast-iron lanterns became available and were occasionally glazed with etched, or coloured glass (*see* illustrations, pp. 70 and 71).

While leaded windows, stained glass, arched windows and bay windows all became part of the Victorian repertoire, the most common remained the wooden window, now simplified to just two, or four large panels of glass. The transition from Georgian-type glazing patterns to the Victorian styles began in the 1830s, although the old-style windows were still being made up until 1850.

The increased size and weight of glass meant that the new windows were slightly sturdier. They often incorporated short lugs or horns on the tops and bottoms of each sash. By 1860 the Georgian style of window was well and truly out of date, and the large plate-glass sashes were *de rigueur*. Victorian houses were built with bay windows and projecting oriel windows as a means of enlarging the room inside and obtaining better views. The bay window was especially popular in coastal areas like Dun Laoghaire and Sandycove where owners of houses wanted to take full advantage of the sea views. Shop-owners also benefited greatly from the glazier's ability to manufacture large sheets of glass, as the new, larger shop windows better displayed their products without a multitude of glazing bars to obscure the view.

The lattice window was often chosen for cottages, gate lodges and churches. This was a cast-iron window that mimicked earlier leaded windows with their small diamond panes. They were often fixed, but sometimes opened on hinges, or on a central pivot.

Moving into the twentieth century, sash windows continued to be popular until the arts and crafts movement of the 1920s began to encourage the use of casement windows again. Wooden casements with rectangular leaded glazing were an attractive feature of early twentieth-century houses, but iron- and steel-framed windows were already becoming widespread in suburban housing.

Stained Glass

Stained glass is a richly decorative field of the applied arts not only because of its wonderful colours but also because of the array of window types and the variety of subject matter. There is almost no intact medieval stained glass in Ireland, unlike the Continent and

England, where every other parish church has such treasures. However, we know that stained glass existed in our medieval monasteries and churches because fragments have been found during archaeological excavations.

Stained-glass windows are composed of small pieces of colour, a mosaic of glass leaded together to tell a story or commemorate a person, or an event. The small, often diamond-shaped pieces of glass, known as quarries, were held together by lead cames or joints. Long ago the quarries were often stained with colour to enrich the dimly lit interiors of medieval churches, the gleaming colours illuminating biblical or religious subjects designed to uplift the spirit. As a result, an ecclesiastical association remains the most common in terms of pre-Renaissance stained-glass art.

During the eighteenth century stained glass was not popular as most of the new churches of the period were Church of Ireland, which were inspired by classical architecture and therefore favoured plain, Georgian-type windows. Exceptions were sometimes made for the east window above the altar, but even here no distraction was permitted to take from the stark spatial and architectural beauty of the building, which was emphasised by its sculptural ornament in wood carving and plasterwork. In houses of the period, stained or coloured glass simply did not feature at all.

The nineteenth-century revival of stained glass coincided with the new interest in the art of the medieval period. Romanesque, Celtic, Gothic, Tudor and Renaissance styles were all copied and reworked. Stained glass, which had occasionally been used in castles and manor houses, found its way into domestic architecture, where it was used on staircases, or perhaps to obscure an ugly view of a back yard. It was also used to celebrate a family name, or for purposes of heraldry, where a crest or motto might be displayed in the appropriate colours. However, by far the greatest number of stained-glass windows were installed in churches. Throughout the nineteenth century, churches of all denominations sprang up in the new suburbs of the city, and were supported by the middle classes and successful merchant patrons who wished to see their names inscribed forever on a stained-glass window. Imported work, such as that by Hardman's of London and Mayer's of Munich, became more commonplace than glass produced in Ireland. It has often been said that the huge volume of nineteenth-century stained glass imported into Ireland from big, almost production-line workshops in England and Germany debased

Opposite page: A stained-glass window from Drimnagh Castle, which displays the heraldic emblem of the Loftus family, the seventeenth-century owners. During restoration of the castle in the 1980s this window was made by Irish Stained Glass Ltd to fit one of the original stone-mullioned openings.
This page
Above: One of a series of stained-glass windows from the staircase of the National Library in Kildare Street, representing famous Renaissance artists.
Bottom: A beautiful stained-glass window from the dairy at Farmleigh House, Castleknock. A series of these windows is incorporated into the front of this ornamental structure, which is located in the garden, near the main house.

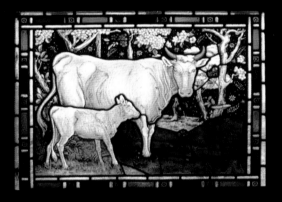

the art form. While it must be accepted that much of this glass did lack originality or any artistic input, it did serve a purpose in purely decorative terms, rather like the yards of cast-iron railings that ornamented the new terraces and houses.

On the domestic front, the Victorians used coloured glass to great effect where it featured in small pieces, and in narrow lengths as a border for large windows, in fanlights, in arched staircase windows and in skylights over stairs and landings. It was also used for internal doors and in glazed porches. Deep cobalt blues, ruby reds, oranges and yellows were favourite colours and special pieces were often acid-etched with stars or vine scrolls. Much of this glass was mass-produced, with transfers being used to add ornamental detail, as is evident from the occasional mistake that can be seen clearly on some windows.

By the 1860s many public buildings of a secular nature, such as the National Library on Kildare Street, and some very grand private houses were using stained glass as an important decorative feature. The National Library and the National Museum were erected in the late 1880s to the designs of Thomas Manly Deane. The Italianate theme he employed is evident in the architecture and in the rich detail of all the decorative finishes, including the stained glass. When Dun Laoghaire Town Hall, a grandiose building in the style of a Venetian palace, was opened with 'great pomp and ceremony' in 1880, the new township's coat of arms was prominently displayed in stained glass over the front door. Private houses, such as Gortmore in Dundrum, which was rebuilt by a wealthy wine merchant in the 1880s, incorporated heraldic motifs into the staircase windows. The Jamesons of distillery fame ordered

---

This page

Above: A stained-glass war memorial window from High School in Rathgar. The figure represents Justice.

Top right: A panel from the window of the staircase of Clanaboy House in Lucan. Such highly decorative and representational stained glass was fashionable in the late Victorian period.

Bottom right: A detail from the stained-glass window of the Rotunda Hospital chapel, which was the gift of entrepreneur Thomas Gresham in the 1860s. This quatrefoil motif, originating in Gothic architecture, was a popular device in ecclesiastical stained glass.

Opposite page

Top left: The colourful stained-glass porch of the Olympia Theatre, Dame Street (formerly called the Empire Palace) was erected around 1900 when a new entrance was created for the theatre. The porch was manufactured by the Saracen Ironworks in Scotland.

Top right: A detail from the famous Harry Clarke windows in Bewley's Café, Grafton Street, showing two exotic birds. These jewel-like windows were among Clarke's finest and last work and were completed in 1928. They were commissioned by Ernest Bewley and are among the few non-religious pieces of stained glass in the city.

Bottom right: Many late Victorian and Edwardian houses in suburban Dublin were decorated with stained glass, especially in and around the front door. This example from Villiers Road, Rathgar, shows the influence of the Art Nouveau style, which was prevalent in the early decades of the twentieth century. The favoured colours for such windows were strong crimson, pink, emerald green and pale blue.

three stained-glass windows, representing the arts, for their town house at Parnell Square, now the Dublin Writers' Museum. Here Music, Painting and Drama are depicted in the style of the Italian Renaissance.

This type of stained glass, though attractive to us now (partly, perhaps, because of its age), was greatly disliked by John Ruskin, William Morris and their followers who sought originality and a return to nature in art. Ruskin, and later Morris, saw the artistic ideal in medieval buildings, especially in Gothic church architecture, and they rejected the entire classical tradition, which they believed to be degenerate and decadent! They elevated the role of the craftsman, such as the carver of wood or stone, and praised the way in which the artisan drew inspiration from nature by observing directly the form of birds, or leaves, or plants. They saw the stylisation of classicism, with its strait-jacketed acanthus leaves and other formalised motifs, as false. There was, however, more than personal aesthetic mores to the design revolution initiated by William Morris. He combined his socialist views and artistic theories to argue against Industrialisation. In his view, mass-produced ornament was flawed because it was a product of capitalisation, made only for the purposes of profit, and it deprived the worker of the craftsman's satisfaction. For Ruskin, it was morally and artistically impoverished. It was the influence of their writings and their work that would eventually bring about the flowering of much original stained-glass art in Ireland in the early twentieth century. The names of Harry Clarke, Evie Hone, the Earley

Studios and Wilhemina Margaret Geddes are just a few of the best-known craftspeople who dominated the revival of artistic stained-glass production.

In the twentieth century the churches and religious orders remained almost the sole patrons of stained-glass artists. Their work continued to glorify religious figures and biblical stories, as it had done since medieval times. There are a few notable exceptions, such as the commission given to Harry Clarke by Ernest Bewley in 1928 to make six windows for his new Grafton Street café. At about this time, Harry Clarke also produced the Geneva window, which illustrates episodes from modern Irish literature. It is on display in the Municipal Gallery of Modern Art. In 1937 Evie Hone created an abstract design for a window in Kimmage Manor, and another piece for the offices of CIÉ on O'Connell Street. Apart from these interesting exceptions, nearly all Irish stained-glass work was of a religious nature.

A vast amount of Victorian stained glass may be seen in the churches of Dublin, but, as we have already noted, most of it was produced outside Ireland. However, *Thom's Street Directory* for 1850 lists five Dublin stained-glass manufacturers, all located in Abbey Street, Marlborough Street and Moore Street. The noted firms of Earley and Powell's, which advertised their wide range of church-decorating arts as early as 1853, combined to produce sculpture, mosaic, metalwork and stained glass from its studios in Camden Street. Thomas Earley trained under the famous Gothic-revival architect Augustus Welby Pugin, while Henry Powell had worked for the English stained-glass company John Hardman and Co. of Birmingham. Earley and Powell's was responsible for many fine stained-glass windows in Dublin churches, for example, St Kevin's Church on Harrington Street.

In the 1860s the main body of St Patrick's Cathedral underwent major refurbishment and rebuilding. This work was sponsored by Sir Benjamin Lee Guinness, who contributed over £150,000 restoring the cathedral. Some of this massive outlay was spent on commissioning the beautiful stained-glass windows. Almost all of the commemorative stained glass in the cathedral was made in the late nineteenth century by English firms, such as Wailes and Co. of Newcastle-upon-Tyne, Burlison and Gryll's, and Heaton, Butler and Bayne of London. In 1864 Wailes and Co. produced the elaborate

Above: A skylight or lantern window from the Pigeon House Hotel in Ringsend. The building was completed by 1795 for the accommodation of mail-packet travellers to England and was a spacious, bright and comfortably furnished building. This skylight is constructed of wood and lead details and has survived intact for over 200 years.

Opposite page

Top: Skylights such as this made an important contribution to the internal lighting of houses, especially in darker areas, such as staircases and landings, in an age before gas or electric light was available.

Bottom: A circular skylight from the staircase of Hazelbrook House in Terenure, now demolished. The petal-like glazing of this metal skylight contained etched glass. This was unusual, and would be found only in an expensively built residence.

large west window of the cathedral, which depicts thirty-nine episodes from the life of St Patrick and the triumph of Christianity over druidism. Some exceptions to the imported work in the cathedral include windows made in the various Dublin workshops of W McBride, J Powell and the Casey Brothers of Moore Street. Nonetheless, St Patrick's Cathedral is the home of the finest collection of English stained glass in Ireland.

Wailes and Co. also produced a remarkable five-light chancel window for the Mariners' Church in Dun Laoghaire (now the home of the National Maritime Museum), which is a copy of the Five Sisters window in York Minster. Replicas of noted medieval works of stained glass were also popular in the nineteenth century. E Bailie of London, the sole exhibitor of stained glass in the Irish Industrial Exhibition of 1853, advertised such pieces as 'Shakespeare reading one of his plays to Queen Elizabeth and her court', and other ornamental works in 'the Norman style'.

Little attention has been devoted to Victorian stained glass of a secular nature, perhaps because much of it lies in private houses and is largely unknown. Among the most interesting examples are the Gothic-style windows of St George's Church in Killiney, produced by Edward Frampton in 1882. The windows depict the owner and his wife at prayer, as well as St George, St Dorothea and the arts, such as Music, Painting and Poetry.

Stone

Stone is the most durable building material known to man, and has been used by people of every century for construction and decoration. It has been used for walls, flooring and outdoor paving, steps, doorcases, entrances, window sills, chimneys, copings, parapets, string courses and sculpture. Dublin is fortunate in that it possesses a large range of interesting stone buildings, representing all periods and styles of architecture. Some of the best-known and least-known examples are illustrated here.

Stone is hard to cut and heavy to move and is therefore an expensive material to work, so its use in a building reflected the cost and status of that structure. A bank, church or other public building will generally be designed and built in stone, and in the eighteenth and nineteenth centuries it was common to find them highly ornamented with carved features and decorative details. The carving of stone added another significant expense to the overall cost because then, as now, stone carving was a skilled and time-consuming activity. It is not unusual to see ornate nineteenth-century Gothic churches in Dublin with unfinished decorative details or missing statuary, no doubt due to an overrun in cost.

In the context of decoration on buildings, stone ornamentation is most usually found in the classical or Gothic traditions. In the classical tradition ornament is provided through the application of the orders – the Doric, Ionic, or Corinthian and their derivatives, Tuscan and Composite. The strict rules and proportions of these orders translated into architecture in the form of columns used, for instance, as porticos, like that of the GPO, or as doorcases, like those of Georgian houses. The classical tradition was thus employed for entrances and gateways, such as in the façade of the Bank of Ireland

Opposite page: The majestic domed interior of Dublin's City Hall displays classical stonework at its finest. It was built as Dublin's Royal Exchange between the years 1768 and 1781, and has recently been returned to its original condition in a major restoration project by Dublin City Council.

This page

Above: This attractive oval window from Rathmines Library displays a very successful example of a terracotta imitation of stone carving. This was made in the early twentieth century when such classical detail in stone and terracotta was popular.

Below right: The Romanesque door of the south transept in Christ Church Cathedral is one of the few remaining examples of medieval carved stonework in the city. Though partially restored in the nineteenth century, much of its original detail in the chevron arches and carved capitals survives.

Opposite page

Top right: A detail from the Castle Street façade of City Hall shows the exuberant carved capitals and stonework carried out by the sculptor Simon Vierpyl in the eighteenth century.

Top left: An inscribed limestone plaque from Huband Bridge on the Grand Canal, near Percy Place, commemorates the date of its erection, 1791, and is a handsome example of Georgian lettering and carved foliage in stone. The bridge with its elegant balustrade and stone details is one of many beautiful small stone bridges which ornamented the Grand and Royal canals, but most of them have been subjected to considerable widening to accommodate modern traffic. This bridge, however, is largely unaltered.

Below right: The eastern entrance to the Custom House, which was designed by James Gandon in 1781. This major public building is widely considered to be the finest classical structure in Ireland and displays some of the most refined stone carving in the country. The massive urn that stands on the parapet was one of Gandon's favourite decorative devices, and gives this wing of the building added emphasis and presence.

on College Green, but it was also applied to the design of decorative features, such as cupolas, fountains and mantelpieces. Carved capitals, sculpted heads and urns are all part of this ancient architectural tradition, the origins of which can be traced back to Greek and Roman sources.

Among the most richly carved stonework of any building in Dublin is that of City Hall, the former Royal Exchange, which stands beside Dublin Castle at the junction of Dame Street, Parliament Street and Cork Hill. The building, completed in 1781, was erected by the merchants of Dublin as an expression of their successful position in city society and of their wealth as traders. This majestic domed structure was entirely constructed of stone and faced on three sides in the giant classical order with cut-stone columns and pilasters. The huge Corinthian capitals, some carved

from single pieces of white Portland stone, are over two-and-a-half feet (1m) high. The frieze and cornices, also of a massive scale, are beautifully carved, as are the roundels which house lion masks. The interior, with its renovated stone floor, is equally impressive and is a perfect example of the marriage of exquisite proportion and architectural ornament.

The type of stone chosen for any building, along with its details, will naturally affect its appearance in terms of texture and colour. The range of building stone in Ireland is chiefly limited to granites, limestones and sandstones, with some marbles and slates. Softer stones that were more easily carved, such as Portland or Caen stone, were imported. The full range of coloured marbles was not available in Ireland, so the traditional white marble was imported from Carrera in Italy, red from Verona and yellow from Siena. However, during the nineteenth century Irish marble quarries were productive and an example of every type to be found in the country may be seen in the columns of the Museum Building in Trinity College, which was erected about 1850.

Granite and limestone were widely used. Granite is still quarried in the Dublin and Wicklow Mountains and was once extracted on a large scale from the Dalkey area in South County Dublin. Granite from these areas was used for most of the city's pavements, a good deal of which are still *in situ*. As it is a coarse, grained igneous rock, granite is not generally suitable for detailed carving.

However, there are some examples of fine decorative sculpture, such as the delightful stone heads of policemen from the Royal Irish Constabulary, which gaze down from Pearse Street Garda Station. They were carved in 1915.

Granite is universally used in Dublin for window sills, coping, string courses, walls and steps. Indeed, the cut-granite steps of old Dublin houses remain an outstanding feature of the city and its craftsmanship. In Victorian times steps were carved with a rounded lip or nose and the walls or plinths that carried railings were often ornamented with subtle mouldings. Rusticated granite was a common feature of the ground floor of some Georgian houses and public buildings, its coarse texture and heavy blockwork lending solidity to the design. This is well exemplified in Merrion Square and on Leinster House. It was usual for the upper floors to be faced in a smoother stone, such as limestone, or sometimes Portland stone, but there are examples of public buildings constructed entirely of granite. Among the most noted of Dublin's public buildings which are faced in granite are the west front of Trinity College, the Rotunda Hospital, the Four Courts and the GPO. Nelson's Pillar and the Wellington Testimonial in the Phoenix Park were also constructed of granite, quarried in Glencullen and Kilgobbin. Other fine examples of granite building include St Paul's Church, Arran Quay, the Pro-Cathedral and the front of the Stock Exchange in Anglesea Street.

Limestone is a smooth, sedimentary rock of pale grey colour and it was quarried in the city itself, in Rathgar — where Jordan's Quarry was noted in the nineteenth century for the toughness of its stone — and from places further afield, such as Clondalkin to the west. Much local Dublin limestone, known as calp, was generally not of sufficiently good quality to be used for dressing as facing stone, or for carving, but was used as rubble for wall-building. Better quality limestone was sourced in quarries in County Meath, such as Ardbraccan. This was used in some eighteenth-century façades, and a fine example can be seen at Charlemont House, begun in 1762 and now the home of the Municipal Gallery of Modern Art. Limestone was more widely used in the nineteenth century for both stone-facing and decorative carving, and it can be seen in many churches, banks and insurance offices of the period. The AIB on Dame Street, for instance, completed in about 1860, is an excellent example of the skilled use of limestone.

Fine examples of carved limestone detail can also be seen in the pilasters of public houses, such as Nugent's, c.1870 (now Bad Bob's), in Essex Street, or O'Rourke's on Main Street, Blackrock. An interesting sculptural group, comprising a dolphin and the sea god Neptune, crowns the corner entrance to the old Dolphin Hotel in Essex Street, now converted for use as a district courthouse. Several impressive licensed premises or pubs built in the late nineteenth century exhibit cut-stone façades, combining limestone and brick. The Stag's Head in Dame Lane, erected in 1895, is a good example.

Gates and Entrances

A wide variety of entrance gates exists throughout the city and county of Dublin. Such gates, from the imposing entrance archways of Dublin Castle to the impressive stucco piers and iron gates of suburban residences, were designed to impress the visitor and to provide security. The three entrances to Dublin Castle were erected in about 1760, and are still in regular use today without any modification. The design of each one is based on the Roman triumphal arch, with a central archway flanked by smaller pedestrian doors. The Cork Hill gate, designed as an arch with a broken pediment, has a matching unused gate to the west of the Bedford Tower. The smaller entrance gate to Tailors' Hall in Back Lane, also with a broken pediment, dates from about 1715 and was built to reflect the status of the Tailors' Guild in Dublin society at that time.

At Powerscourt House in South William Street, the large town house of the Wingfield family, a pair of impressive stone-built arches once gave access to and from the courtyard and stables at the rear of the house, an area now converted into a shopping centre.

The former archbishop's palace, St Sepulchre's (now Kevin Street Garda Station), boasted tall gate piers, as did the Provost's House at Trinity College. These piers not only provided support for the heavy

wrought-iron gates that stood there but also delineated the private space belonging to the archbishop and provost. It was common for the stone gate piers to be a feature in themselves, often classical in style, sometimes Gothic or Italianate, and varying in complexity. There might be two or more piers, sometimes a sweep or curved wall and perhaps a pedestrian gate, too.

Long ago, every detached house in County Dublin had its own avenue, a handsome pair of gates and possibly a gate lodge. Georgian gate piers were usually built in courses of cut-stone or ashlar and were usually topped with a generous cap stone surmounted by balls, pineapples, or sometimes urns. By contrast, the piers of Victorian entrances were often made from single blocks of granite, sometimes featuring a recessed panel. Circular piers with rounded caps also became popular, examples of which may be seen in nineteenth-century residential areas, such as Monkstown, Clontarf, or Rathgar. Even the smaller granite piers of more modest houses are a noteworthy aspect of the whole heritage of antique stonework.

Carving

As one begins to notice the decorative details of Dublin City, it is clear that stone has been used for centuries to ornament buildings and to provide lettering and numbers. Stone carving appears in many guises, from the largest coats of arms and friezes to the humblest name plaques. In the grandest public buildings the stonemason's craft was displayed to the full, with carved figures occupying the pediments, as over the main entrance to the Custom House, or standing aloft on pedestals and gateways, as on the College of Surgeons. Name plaques constituted another branch of the stonecutter's craft. A small stone plaque inscribed with the name Heytesbury Street and a hand with a pointing forefinger dates from 1832 and indicates the street name. A dramatic example of lettering in stone is the name and date of Westmoreland Lock, carved into the wall of one of the locks of the Grand Canal at Ringsend.

Some of the most unusual examples of stonework in Dublin belong to the classical tradition. The language of classical architectural details contains many curious features, such as the use of rusticated stone, whose blockwork was used in the lower floors of façades to suggest weight and strength. Vermiculated stonework was similarly used, its deeply gouged hollows and holes were carved in imitation of great blocks of fossilised stone eaten away by worms. One of the most striking pieces of carving in this style appears over the formidable entrance to Kilmainham Jail and incorporates deadly-looking serpents into its contorted design: a symbol of evil made all the more

menacing by the darkness of its north-facing aspect.

During the nineteenth century the range of decorative stone carving on buildings widened as a penchant for more eclectic styles of architecture became apparent. Features from Egyptian temples, French Gothic cathedrals, English Tudor mansions, Flemish Renaissance town houses and even Celtic traditions made their way into various buildings of the Victorian period. At that time a new interest in naturalistic representation evolved in stone carving, with panels of fruit and flowers, or string courses of leaves and foliage quite recognisable as those of vines, or oaks. Realistic carvings of heads, both animal and human, became popular on Gothic churches, banks, offices and business premises of all kinds. There can have been few more demanding tasks for the sculptor than that of carving a full coat of arms, including a pile of trophies and weapons, like the one that can be seen over the entrance to the Bank of Ireland in Foster Place.

The tradition of stone carving did not entirely vanish in the twentieth century, although such detail was seldom employed on buildings after 1930. During the rebuilding of Sackville (now O'Connell) Street following its almost complete destruction in 1916, stone was specified for the façades of all new buildings. The architecture of the street boasts a fine display of decorative features, such as the sphinxes on the Gresham Hotel, wreaths on Clery's, urns on the building of the Permanent TSB, a lion mask on the Bank of Ireland and a ram's head on Clarke's shoe shop. The imperial grandeur of the present Government Buildings on Merrion Street, completed in 1922 as a College of Science, was finished entirely in cut stone, including much excellent sculptural detail, by the firm of CW Harrison of Pearse Street.

Sculptural ornament of a symbolic nature made an occasional appearance in the 1940s and 1950s, with examples like the Government's Department of Trade and Industry building in Kildare Street, or the Post Office on Andrew Street.

Other examples of twentieth-century ornamentation in stone include work at Holles Street National Maternity Hospital on Merrion Square, the Gas Company buildings in Hawkins Street and Pearse Street Garda Station. A beautifully sculpted child's head appears over the main entrance (no longer in use) to Holles Street Hospital. This piece, carved in limestone, dates from 1936. A similar example may be seen in the head of a goat on the early twentieth-century premises of the Ulster Bank at the corner of Baggot Street and Pembroke Street.

Doorcases

The front door of any building is its functional and symbolic entrance. It provides both a point of welcome and a means of security. It is the physical barrier between the public world of the street and the private world within. The great variety and number of doors and entrances that may be seen in Dublin is an integral part of the city's architectural heritage, though they are taken for granted by many of the inhabitants of the capital. On a daily basis, people lock and unlock thousands of doors, some of which are over 250 years old, and pass through these entrances, which have witnessed so much history.

In times past, the doors of a castle or a fortified house had a defensive aspect and were solidly built of strongly backed vertical

timbers. The doors could be secured from the inside with heavy bolts or beams of wood. Such doors were sometimes simple pedestrian entrances but were more usually of double width, capable of admitting a cart or carriage. Up until the seventeenth century they were generally made of oak – the commonest and strongest timber then available in Ireland. No medieval doors are known to exist in Dublin, although a pair of internal doors in St Sepulchre's, now Kevin Street Garda Station, provides an ornate example from the seventeenth century. One example of an ancient door survives in St Patrick's Cathedral, but it is now on display rather than in use.

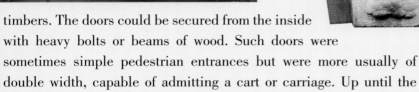

THE TURNSTONE

Most house-owners, even those occupying the most humble abode, use the front entranceway to provide some distinctive feature that marks off their home from others. This can be achieved either in the colour of the door, or in ornamentation, such as brickwork, about the entrance. Front doors were generally painted in dark colours, but in Ireland a taste developed for using a wide variety of colours, including bright ones. In a grander residence, or more important building the doorcase provided an elaborate frame for the door, which expressed the status or wealth of the owner. Elaborate carved stonework, pillars, panelled doors and fanlight windows can all be used to great artistic and decorative effect. Nowhere is this better

Opposite page

Top right: The figure of Science from the pediment of Government Buildings, erected in 1913.

Top left: A collection of chained serpents writhe over the entrance to Kilmainham Jail.

Middle (first): A menacing griffon from the Unitarian Church in St Stephen's Green.

Middle (second): A 'Green Man'-type sculpture from All Saints' Church in Raheny.

Bottom: This unicorn, carved in Portland stone for the roofline of the Custom House, is shown here under repair.

This page

Top far left: A gilded limestone dolphin disporting itself over the entrance to the former Dolphin Hotel in Essex Street.

Top middle: This strange figure graced the North British and Mercantile Insurance Company building (now Eason's bookstore) on the corner of Nassau Street and Dawson Street.

Top far right: A representation of the River Foyle is one of the striking riverine heads or keystones from the Custom House, representing the river gods of Ireland. These majestic carvings were the work of the talented Edward Smyth. Each head carries a symbol of the land it flows through, here, the walls of Derry.

Above middle: A small oval plaque, on the front of a Georgian house in Baggot Street, represents the turnstone, a sea bird noted for its ability to investigate. It was used as the symbol for an office of the Revenue Commissioners! This twentieth-century piece is beautifully carved in limestone.

Left: A classical-style panel from the west front of the King's Inns on Constitution Hill. The figures represent *Wisdom*, *Justice* and *Prudence*, attended by *Truth*, *Time* and *History*.

This page

Below: Dublin's Georgian streetscapes are characterised by the variety and richness of their door surrounds. This example from Molesworth Street, dating from the middle of the eighteenth century, is derived from the architecture of James Gibbs and incorporates a stone architrave with blockwork and a bold keystone. The door itself is not of the period.

Opposite page

Top right: The Huguenot Cemetery in Merrion Row possesses an elegantly proportioned Gothic door that is part of an alcove on the back wall. During the nineteenth century the Gothic style became the predominant idiom in all church and religious architecture.

Bottom right: A Victorian doorcase in Palmerston Park. In contrast to the Georgian period, Victorian doorcases took many forms, including the Romanesque or Italianate style, which can be seen here. Such entrances, composed of a cut-stone arch, were supported by pillars of polished granite or marble pillars.

executed than in such places as Merrion Square, with its rows of elegant eighteenth-century doors, all in harmony but each slightly different.

Dublin has an impressive stock of cut-stone doorcases, the earliest of which date from the 1730s. These, however, are rare as many examples have disappeared and are now known only from photographs. A few beautifully proportioned early doorcases may be seen in Dublin Castle, but one of the most interesting is that of 10 Mill Street, which still exists though it is no longer *in situ*. This extremely elegant and tall doorcase, probably erected in the 1720s on a merchant's house in the Liberties, has fluted columns, richly carved capitals and a broken swan-neck pediment. The oldest cut-stone doorcases made use of simple classical architraves or mouldings and tended to be tall and narrow.

By the 1740s a new type of arched doorcase was in fashion, in which the architrave was broken by prominent blockwork. This type was commonly called a Gibbsian doorcase after the eighteenth-century architect James Gibbs, whose published designs made it so popular in homes of modest scale and type. The Gibbs-style doorcase remained in fashion until 1760 and even later, and can be seen in all parts of the city and county. It was generally constructed of granite, which would normally have been painted, and it was accompanied by simple timber fanlights and doors, with up to nine raised panels. There are good examples in Ranelagh, Blackrock and on medium-sized detached houses dating from about 1750.

The strength of the front door was as important as its attractive appearance, and by the eighteenth century most were panelled, with solid horizontal, or lozenge-shaped boards lining the back. As oak gave way to pine, it became usual to paint doors as the knots in pine could not otherwise be fully weatherproofed.

Most of the large doorcases created between 1750 and 1770 were made of limestone and even though they were painted, the chiselling of the stone is still clearly visible. Most of these are Doric or Tuscan, and many incorporate a small fanlight with a broken pediment. The use of Portland stone became more widespread during the last two decades of the eighteenth century, its fine grain making it very suitable for carved detail. The best examples are to be found on Merrion Square. The grandest houses made use of the full classical orders, complete with columns, capitals, frescoes and pediments. Excellent examples can be seen on the palatial houses of

St Stephen's Green and Henrietta Street. The great height of the stone doorcases of 14 and 15 St Stephen's Green is only obvious when a person stands beside the doors. Their scale is dictated by the size and height of the building.

The Mill Street doorcase mentioned previously is one of the earliest examples of the use of engaged columns on a house in Dublin. Most Georgian doorcases built subsequently employed engaged or three-quarter columns, which is to say they were not free-standing or fully circular but were attached to the wall behind. The columns, which were made of at least three separate pieces (the base, shaft and capital) were held together by means of square wooden pegs and were fixed to the wall with iron cramps and lead.

The most common Georgian doorcase in Dublin was fitted into a recessed, arched opening with a moulded stone reveal. It had simple Ionic columns supporting a heavy stone lintel, which was usually carved. A fanlight was fitted to the semicircular brick arch above and all of the stonework and the fanlight was painted. These are the typical doors which ornament the houses of late eighteenth-century Dublin, and can be seen on the streets and squares of the city. The variations found in such doors on grander and more expensive houses often include sidelights, to allow more light into the hallway, and this wider type of doorcase led to greater elaboration in the design, with double columns or a pair of columns and pilasters. There are many fine examples on Merrion Square, North Great George's Street and Parnell Square.

These Georgian doors, so much an emblem of Dublin, are the most elaborate decorative feature on the otherwise restrained façades of the houses. They are almost universally made of Portland stone, a fine, easily carved white limestone that was quarried at Portland in the south of England. The quarries at Portland are still being mined and the easily worked stone is still available. During the restoration of the Custom House some years ago, matching stone was sourced there.

The well-known sculptor Simon Vierpyl had workshops at Bachelor's Walk, and though he is recorded as having made statues and many important pieces of sculpture for public buildings it is probable that his bread-and-butter work included carving decorative doorcases and stone chimney pieces.

Some doorcases, such as that at 40 Dominick Street, exhibit elaborate stone carving. In this case, the frieze above the sidelights is decorated with garlands of leaves, roses and flowers hung from small rings. The style of carving is similar to the plasterwork ornament found in other houses of the 1760s. Some doorcases of the 1770s have a coved or splayed arch, which was decorated in stucco

or compo (an outdoor stucco). A good example may be seen at 35 North Great George's Street, where sphinxes are incorporated into the design.

As in all aspects of style, the transition from Georgian to Victorian was a gradual one and many of the characteristics of the eighteenth-century doorcase lived on well into the 1840s. This involved the standard arched opening with the persistent use of columns and fanlights. The new Victorian terraces of Dublin's suburbs, such as Rathmines and Blackrock, consisted of smaller houses that were more cheaply built than their early city counterparts but which still displayed an essentially Georgian doorcase. Stone was replaced with less expensive timber, and designs often adopted the neo-classical style with fluted columns. For instance, many of the new terraces in Dun Laoghaire, such as George's Street and De Vesci Terrace, have Doric-style timber doorcases. Some unusual variations occur, such as the unorthodox example in Pleasants Street (off Camden Street) with bizarre 'Egyptian'-style capitals.

In the early nineteenth-century, painted render or cement was the favoured treatment, instead of brick, for façades on coastal terraces, and the painted wooden doorcases blended in perfectly. By the 1840s a new style was becoming fashionable as timber columns gave way to timber pilasters with carved brackets supporting an entablature. Gradually the style of the hall door changed as the typical two- or four-panelled Victorian front door emerged. The recessed Victorian panels were bordered by simpler but heavier rounded mouldings.

Later in the nineteenth century the columns and pilasters disappeared in favour of brick-arched entrances and porches. Typically, the door was comprised of just two long panels, sometimes arched, sometimes rectangular. Various terraces and squares were built in the suburbs during the 1880s and after, such as Dartmouth and Grosvenor squares in Dublin 6, Eaton Square in Monkstown and Lindsay Road in Glasnevin, which characterise the later Victorian style. The hall door was recessed, providing space for a small tiled porch, and stained glass began to be used in the window above the door and in the sidelights.

In the 1890s and on into the Edwardian period it became common to replace the upper panels of the door with stained glass and sometimes cast-iron panels. Decorative entrances incorporating lozenge and dog-tooth patterns, using yellow, red and even purple brick, became usual in Victorian houses. Gothic variations, as can be seen on Terenure Road East, were also popular.

Paving

On account of the poor condition of many of Dublin's pavements, or complete lack of them in places, an Act was passed by Parliament in 1774 to regulate the paving of the city's 'streets, quays, bridges, squares, yards, courts and alleys'. Since that time most of Dublin's pavements have been surfaced with slabs of granite, much of it from quarries in the Dublin Mountains. The granite of the Dalkey and Dun Laoghaire area was generally considered to be harder and more durable than that of Wicklow, but the later stone was more easily worked and thus was cheaper. Following the surfacing of the city's streets, the owners of houses and business premises took care to keep them clean and free from obstruction. The 'antique pavement', as it has been called, not only remains very serviceable but is also an important aspect of the city's historic streetscapes.

Though much was lost initially through careless roadworks by service providers of gas, electricity and telephone lines, over the last twenty years Dublin City Council has made a point of preserving these original kerbs and pavements, wherever possible. At the same time, much new granite paving has also been laid, in keeping with the 'antique pavement', in areas like Temple Bar, the Docklands and elsewhere in the city.

Pages 84-85, three pictures: Before the advent of modern building material, such as concrete, stone was the principal building material and was used not only for houses and public buildings but also for harbours, bridges, pavements, walls, steps and decorative detail. Dublin is particularly fortunate in having a sizeable portion of its antique granite pavements intact. Fine examples of granite pavements may be seen at Merrion Square, City Hall and St Patrick's Close (*top*), and at many other locations. The stone used comes from the Dublin granite range and was quarried in Dalkey, Ticknock and other small quarries. By contrast, the stone setts (*left*) with which many of the city's streets were paved in the nineteenth century were sourced from England and Scotland, and are a particularly hard type of stone. In recent years Dublin City Council has resurfaced certain areas of the city with stone setts, for example, Temple Bar, Smithfield and other areas, thus greatly enhancing the visual quality of the city. *Above* is Dun Laoghaire harbour, an outstanding example of the use of granite as a structural material. The harbour, one of the largest artificial harbours in Europe, was constructed between the years 1815 and 1850 and consumed thousands of tonnes of granite from the Dalkey quarry. Many of the cut-stone details, such as the steps, harbour buildings and piers, are beautifully finished.

Fanlights

If Dublin is famous for any one decorative feature it must be the beautiful Georgian doors with their delicate fanlights which line the eighteenth-century squares and streets of the city. The doors of Merrion Square or Mountjoy Square were, almost without exception, embellished by fanlights of the most intricate and elaborate designs. These examples are some of the largest in Dublin City. However, many houses, especially Georgian villas in County Dublin, made use of even larger and wider fanlights, as, for example, at Delaford in Firhouse, now demolished. And while fanlights are mainly to be found in houses, there are examples in public buildings too, such as the Custom House.

Fanlights (the name describes its fan-shaped structure) originated out of the need to illuminate an otherwise dark hallway, while incorporating its design into the overall architectural scheme of the entrance. In those days natural light, or the use of candles or oil lamps were the only means of lighting the darker parts of houses, such as the hallways. What is quite remarkable about these semicircular or elliptical windows is that, like snowflakes, one seldom finds two that are identical. Each one is unique because each fanlight was handmade. The doorcase and the fanlight formed the focal point and showpiece of the house frontage.

The first fanlights were of solid timber construction, the glazing bars radiating out from a central point, not unlike the spokes of a cartwheel. The glazing bars were frequently curved to create a Gothic or pointed arch, an example of which may be seen at the Rotunda Hospital. These wooden fanlights date from between 1710 and 1760 and were common in the plain arched doorways of the houses of that period. They were once to be found all over the city, especially in the older Georgian districts where the houses dated from 1730 to 1760, such as South

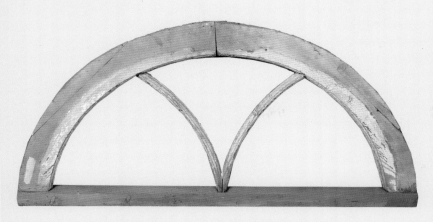

Opposite page
Top left: The graceful front entrance to Riversdale House, Palmerstown, with its magnificent fanlight, is a fine example of this decorative feature which can be seen all over Dublin City and county. The fanlight is designed to fill the semicircular arch above the door and its traceried glass lights the hall inside. The ornamental sidelights on this entrance also illuminate the interior of the hall.
Bottom left: A coloured fanlight from Dun Laoghaire, *c.*1840. During the early nineteenth century coloured fanlights became popular and were much used in the internal halls of houses.

This page
Top left: An early timber fanlight, of simple construction, from a house dated around 1740–1750. It illustrates the beginning of this type of window, with its simple early origins, before the elaborate and complex designs of the late Georgian period. Such simple fanlights were commonplace in modest houses in Fownes Street, Temple Bar.
Bottom right: This Gothic-style fanlight from the early nineteenth century comes from a terrace of late Georgian-style brick houses in Upper Rathmines Road. The Gothic idiom was fashionable for decorative features for a short time in the early 1800s.
Bottom left: A tear-drop fanlight from Westland Row, *c.*1840. While people associate the fanlight with the Georgian period, it did in fact remain popular in domestic architecture for more than a century, and there are many examples to be found in Dublin's Victorian suburbs, such as Clontarf, Rathmines and Dun Laoghaire.

Frederick Street, Fownes Street and Capel Street. This architectural feature was not confined to the most fashionable districts, and was once as commonplace on the quays of the River Liffey as in any other part of the city. Examples can be found in districts as far apart as Dorset Street, Camden Street, Temple Bar and the Liberties. Many houses adorned by such fanlights were cleared away during the past thirty years, and most of the fanlights were simply destroyed.

During the latter half of the eighteenth century, timber fanlights became more delicate, resulting in a refined spider's-web effect made up of the thinnest strips of wood. The bent element was tacked and puttied into place. Ornaments formed from gesso or putty were attached to various joints or extremities, and included urns, rosettes and heads. Gesso beads fixed to strong thread were glued to the timber's glazing bars. An example of these are the fanlights on Leeson Street. After more than 200 years, these timber fanlights are usually heavily overpainted so that the thinness of the structure is not apparent, and the refinement of the detail is almost invisible.

In some houses, usually larger ones, sidelights were added at each side of the door and these were also made of wood with similar gesso ornamentation. Such sidelights presented a security risk to the house and were often protected internally by a wrought-iron grille, or a shutter, or both. In some cases decorative iron grilles were also placed behind the fanlight to provide additional security.

From the 1770s onwards delicate, almost frail-looking fanlights were constructed in metal and faced with lead ornamentation. The designs of Robert Adam and other architects of the period utilised neo-classical elements in refined details, such as rosettes, garlands, swags and small urns. The ornaments were cast in lead and soldered on to lead cames, and those were attached to a thin iron, or sometimes zinc structure. This metal structure was fastened to a semicircular

87

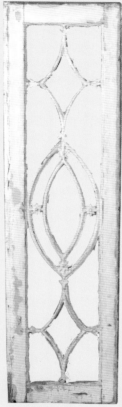

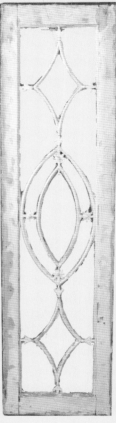

wooden frame, which in turn was fitted to the brick arch of the doorway.

Fanlights were generally painted in an off-white or stone colour, similar to the doorcase below, so that the decorative design stood out against the background of dark glass and brickwork. They were especially popular in the terraced houses and villas of the 1820s and 1830s, when front doors were decorated with columns and approached by a flight of granite steps, thus forming the chief decorative feature of the house. Lead fanlights remained popular in Dublin houses right up until the 1840s, and many examples can be seen in the suburbs – Dun Laoghaire, Blackrock, Howth and Lucan. Fanlights appear in the grandest mansions, such as Lucan House, and in the humblest farmhouses, gate lodges and even cottages. Designs include petal forms, tear-drops and anthemions, as well as the better-known spider's-web shape.

Although the semicircular fanlight is the most well-known feature of Dublin's Georgian streetscapes, they were sometimes made in rectangular or even oval shapes. A good example of the rectangular fanlight, composed of crossed arrows and an oval, is to be seen in Molesworth Street, where it forms part of Whytes shopfront. Another interesting rectangular window may also be seen on Bachelor's Walk, comprising four circles. Certain regional characteristics developed in fanlight-making, for instance, in Clonmel and parts of Munster the circle and oval is a favoured motif, but it is rare in Dublin. A number of fanlights were designed with oil lanterns incorporated so that the hallway and doorstep were simultaneously lit at night. Examples include York Road, Dun Laoghaire, and 35 North Great George's Street.

Catalogues exist for some English fanlight-makers of the late eighteenth century, but it seems certain that most of these delicate artefacts were made locally. The skill involved in their making and glazing would have been easily accomplished by the many cabinet-makers in eighteenth-century Dublin. Furthermore, the transport of such a delicate artefact from England would have posed many problems in the eighteenth century.

Designs for Sackville Street (now O'Connell Street) drawn up by the Wide Streets Commission in the early nineteenth century indicate shopfronts which incorporate fanlights over their entrance doors. These fanlights, fitted to rectangular spaces, are similar to the restored example at 4 Castle Street, the home of the Dublin Civic Trust. No doubt the published designs of Robert Adam (1770s) and English fanlight-maker Joseph Bottomley (c.1795) provided inspiration for the Dublin manufacturers who were, in any case, very inventive and produced an unending variety of designs.

The use of coloured glass was rare before 1830, as all fanlights were glazed with delicate, clear glass that was hand-blown. At this time the production of glass was exclusively handmade, and irregularities in thickness and colour were commonplace. In some instances fanlight glass was as thin as eggshell, and often the curve of the concentric circles of the glass-blower's disc can still be seen. Known as crown glass, such original glazing gives subtle reflections to an original fanlight.

By the 1830s the use of coloured glass had crept into fashion, and by the middle of the nineteenth century acid-etched glass and coloured panes were the norm in fanlights, which were now being used internally in hallways, on staircases and landings, too. Stars and rosettes and trailing vine tendrils appear in bright orange, crimson red, ultramarine blue and deep yellow-coloured glass.

Opposite page: A large fanlight with its accompanying sidelights from a demolished villa in Sandymount. This spider's-web pattern, from the 1830s, was one of the most frequently used designs and can be seen in Merrion Square and elsewhere.

Above: A more robust style of fanlight remained in use until the middle of the nineteenth century, as seen here on a house in Monkstown. The narrower sidelights have been simplified to a series of roundels.

Plasterwork

The tradition of applying decorative plasterwork to the walls and ceilings of buildings goes back to the Egyptians, if not before. The Romans made use of plaster gypsum, a mixture of marble dust and slaked lime, to decorate the interiors of their houses and public buildings. In Ireland, our medieval cathedrals, abbeys and castles were also plastered and sometimes decorated with fresco paintings and, on occasion, with relief designs in plasterwork. Unfortunately, we have little to show from these early times, though written accounts record the existence of decorated rooms in Dublin's old Tholsel, a public building and meeting place that once stood opposite Christ Church Cathedral.

The quantity and quality of decorative plasterwork in Dublin is unrivalled by any other European city. The extraordinary mantelpiece from Old Bawn House in Tallaght, which is in the National Museum (*see* illustration, p.123), is the work of stucco plasterers and is dated 1635. This rare piece of plasterwork shows how accomplished early sculptural work of this kind could be and how most of it was at that time modelled by hand, which remained the practice well into the second half of the eighteenth century. An example of the early compartmental ceiling, made in papier mâché and composed of many heavy frames richly ornamented with fruit and flowers, may be seen in the restored chapel at the Royal Hospital, Kilmainham.

The flowering of this kind of architectural ornament as an art form in its own right reached a peak of originality during the mid-eighteenth century. Decorative plasterwork progressed through a series of styles, each one beautiful but different. It began in the late

Opposite page: The hallway of Belfield House (1790), which gives its name to the campus of University College, Dublin. This example of late eighteenth-century plasterwork illustrates the great delicacy and beauty of plasterwork for the creation of decorative interiors. The absidal recesses of the hall are lavishly covered with delicate ornamentation.

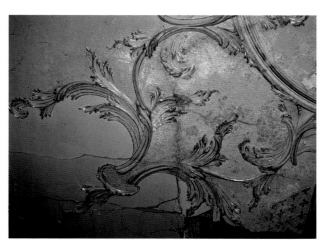

seventeenth century and early 1700s with bold, compartmentalised designs, which were favoured by the Palladian architects, like Pearce who designed the Parliament House (now Bank of Ireland) in College Green. The three-dimensional plasterwork of the chapel in the Rotunda Hospital is the work of the Swiss-Italian stuccodore Bartholomew Cramillion, who introduced a new bold style of figurative plasterwork to Ireland in the late 1750s. His life-size figures, cherubs and swags of fruit are almost free-standing and seem unattached to the ceiling itself. It is a masterpiece of composition and modelling.

By the mid-eighteenth century the rococo style had become popular with stuccodores like Robert West, who was trained in the Dublin Society Schools, leading the field. The plasterwork of his own house at 20 Dominick Street is probably the most outstanding achievement of that period, exhibiting birds and foliage in high relief. The term rococo is derived from the word *rocaille*, a scallop shell-like ornament arranged in great C-shaped flourishes and enriched with flowing acanthus leaves. Even the ceilings of quite modest houses in Leeson Street, South Frederick Street and Parliament Street (dating from the 1740s and

1750s) were sometimes decorated in this way, though few examples now remain.

This style – a free-flowing approach to ornament that has been described as a form of Baroque decoration – was made popular between 1730 and 1760. At about this time too, classical subjects began to be introduced, using figures from well-known myths and fables. Juno and Antigone, Minerva and the warrior, and Mercury are some of the exquisite subjects the La Francini brothers modelled for 9 St Stephen's Green in about 1756. Aesop's *Fables* provided the inspiration for the Fox and the Stork, so beautifully carried out in about 1752 on a gilded ceiling and now residing in Áras an Uachtaráin.

After the 1780s, the art of the stuccodore was dominated by the delicate but low-relief geometric designs of Robert Adam and his followers. The ceilings of this late Georgian period, though very pretty and decorative, lacked the originality and sculptural vigour of the mid-eighteenth century.

Many stuccodores worked as a family concern, such as Robert and John West, and Michael and George Stapleton. Charles Thorp was another noted stuccodore whose work may be seen in North Great George's Street. Michael Stapleton was one of the most accomplished stuccodores of the late eighteenth century, and his work reflects the prevalent taste for the Adam style. Stapleton decorated some of the principal rooms of Powerscourt House in 1777 using a wide repertoire of classical detail –

dancing figures, copied originally from a Roman sarcophagus, delicate urns, fans, thin scrolls of foliage, cherubs and medallions. Similar work was to be found in large County Dublin houses, such as Newlands House (Clondalkin) and Rosemount (Clonskeagh), both demolished during the 1980s, and in Belfield House, still standing and giving its name to the UCD campus.

Stapleton carried out a large number of contracts in houses on St Stephen's Green and North Great George's Street. Among the most sophisticated compositions and most delicate of Stapleton's work are the many ceilings in 17 St Stephen's Green (the Kildare Street and University Club) and Lucan House. In Lucan House, even the walls of the drawing room are decorated with symmetrical 'Adamesque' ornaments, which are perfectly matched in the design of the door surrounds and marble mantelpiece.

Stapleton often incorporated musical instruments, such as flutes, French horns and violins, into his decorative schemes for what was very much the fashion at the time – the music room. Number 52 St Stephen's Green and Belvedere House are both good examples. Belvedere House, the home of Belvedere College since 1875, is probably Stapleton's most lavish work, and was completed in 1785. Scarcely a square foot of the walls or ceiling of the staircase, hall and landing remains undecorated. The library features panels of animals associated with the hunt, such as the stag, hound and fox. Stapleton's refined approach is also in evidence in the ceiling of what is now the Senate Chamber in Leinster House, completed in the early 1790s, and in the beautiful semi-vaulted ceilings of the Exam Hall and Chapel in Trinity College, completed in the 1770s.

The Stuccodore's Trade

The best plaster was made from gypsum (burnt limestone), or from plaster of Paris. The plasterer's skill was as much in demand in previous centuries as it is today. The work of the ordinary plasterer involved skimming the walls and ceilings of houses with several coats, first of lime mortar mixed with animal hair for strength, then of plaster or gypsum to produce a smooth finish. The plasterer would also

This page

Above: A plaster peach from a lost eighteenth-century ceiling on St Stephen's Green West, seen from behind and showing its wooden armature with which it was fixed to the ceiling.

Right: A fragment of decorative plaster from Kenure Park, Rush, County Dublin. Kenure was demolished in the 1970s. Such details as this acroterion, derived from Greek architecture, were part of the repertoire of the neo-classical style.

Below: A boldly modelled piece of plaster from the nineteenth century that was salvaged from the ruins of Frascati House, Blackrock.

Bottom: An acorn detail from the original Four Courts building, destroyed by fire in 1922. The Four Courts, with its noble dome, was designed by James Gandon and built in the last decade of the eighteenth century.

Opposite page

Top right: A ceiling from Rathfarnham Castle. The castle was modernised in 1770–1771 to the designs of James Stewart, the noted Georgian architect. The ornate ceilings in the Gilt room incorporate circular panels and compartments of refined plasterwork.

Bottom: From the frieze in the ballroom of the now-vanished Newlands House, Clondalkin, come this pair of dancing ladies. The design was inspired by an ancient Roman sarcophagus and was a favourite device of the Stapleton stuccodores who are believed to have carried out the decorative plasterwork in the house.

have been able to run cornices around the rooms, at the junction of the walls and ceiling, using a variety of classical models.

The plaster ceiling was applied to a grid of oak laths, which were nailed to the underside of the floor joists. Three coats at least were given to a wall, or ceiling. The laths were generally made from the riven heart oak, that is, the wood at the heart of a bough or piece of oak. Cow or bullock hair was generally added to the plaster to give it strength, although goat hair was sometimes used for the finer top coat. These three styles of plastering were known in Dublin as lath-scratched, floated and coated. It was a messy and arduous job as wet plaster is heavy to mix, carry and apply. Many plasterers had an appetite for alcohol and their lives were often shortened by the habit of hard work and drinking too much!

Stuccodores (or decorative plasterers), on the other hand, could demand far higher wages than those who did straight work, and we know from various accounts that their skills were not bought cheaply. Robert West was paid almost £1,000 for cornices and plasterwork in the Rotunda Hospital in 1756, a huge sum at that time.

The stuccodore's craft fell into two main categories: freehand and cast. One-off pieces were generally hand-modelled *in situ*, sometimes on a scaffold under the ceiling. Repeated ornament, such as rosettes, egg-and-dart, or dentils, were cast on a bench in the room below, probably by an assistant. Stuccodores would have kept a store of models or casts, which could be reused for other jobs. These included urns, medallions and masks. They might spend time during the winter months in their own workshops, turning out large quantities of small details and other ornamental elements.

Earlier ornaments in the rococo style, of which a good deal survives in Dublin, were generally fixed to the ceiling or cornice by means of an armature, usually a thin piece of oak, or a nail. Pieces of wire and canvas were used for larger objects. The decorative piece, such as a peach, or a flower, was pushed into the setting plaster of the ceiling with its armature firmly embedded. Panels, plaques and other similar pieces of cast detail

were scratched or scored on the reverse so as to provide a key when fixing them into position. From the 1760s onwards the great majority of decorative plasterwork was made up of cast elements, which particularly suited the more geometric and repetitive style of Robert Adam. As we have already noted when discussing ironwork, Adam's published designs did much to influence all decorative work in the late eighteenth century. There are many examples of this delicate type of stucco in Dublin, such as the ceilings in Powerscourt House, South William Street, or at 35 and 38 North Great George's Street. All of the rooms on the ground floor of Lucan House are exquisitely decorated in this manner.

The stuccodore's toolkit contained trowels, knives and spatulas for working the plaster, but also rulers, squares, compasses and scales for setting out their designs. Most plasterers were equipped with wooden tressels on which to work, and ladders and scaffolding were needed to gain access to and allow ease of movement at ceiling level. A quantity of troughs and tubs would also have been necessary to mix the plaster and to carry slaked lime, water and sand. As fresh plaster sets rather quickly, the stuccodore would sometimes mix it with glue, sour milk, or even beer in order to delay the process and give himself more

time to model. Frost
adversely affects the setting
of plaster, so plasterers were
unable to work much during the winter
months.

It is worth remembering that most ceilings which are decorated
with plasterwork are at least twelve feet (3.5m), or even fifteen
feet (4.5m) in height, and that the stuccodore's intention
was to create an overall decorative scheme with specific
high points of interest. Even though it is not usual to
examine such plaster at close-quarters, it is remarkable
how much attention was given to every detail and to the
overall finish. Unfortunately, the layers of paint accumulated
over the centuries frequently obscure all detail, although in
recent years much of the best plasterwork in Dublin has been
carefully cleaned and now looks quite spectacular.

The question is frequently asked: what were the original colours of
these eighteenth-century ceilings? The present trend is for white, off-
white, pale greys and a little gilding, but there is evidence that some
original ceilings were brightly painted with a palette of oranges,
blues, greens, reds and golds, inspired by the brightly tinted wall

Pages 96-97

Top: Four panels representing musical instruments from the frieze of the ballroom in Newlands House, Clondalkin. The use of such instruments as decorative emblems was widespread in ceilings in the eighteenth century, especially in rooms used for musical and dancing entertainments.

Page 96, bottom left: A classical urn and anthemion design from the ceiling of Swords House. This type of refined classical detail was inspired by excavations in places such as Pompeii and was popularised by designers such as Robert Adam.

This page

Group of six, top right: A collection of original, mid-eighteenth-century decorative features from 60 St Stephen's Green, whose three plasterwork ceilings, though lost, were copied and replaced in the building in the 1980s. These boldly modelled, free-hand pieces display the excellent skill of Dublin's stuccodores.

Above right: Three fragments from the drawing room and ceiling of 15 Parnell Square, where rococo plasterwork was dismantled in the early 1980s. The use of grapes and other fruits, as well as roses, was one of the most frequently used elements in ceiling design.

paintings which were then being excavated in places like Pompeii and Herculaneum in Italy. The richly decorated interior of Belvedere House, with its bright blues, pinks and oranges, may seem a little garish to the more restrained taste of our times, but it was all in vogue in the 1960s when groups like the Irish Georgian Society were trying to research original styles and raise awareness about this aspect of our heritage in order to rescue it from the wrecker's ball.

While some of the houses which contained fine examples of the eighteenth-century stuccodores' art were demolished, ceilings were sometimes saved by being dismantled and recreated elsewhere. The stunning ceilings of Mespil House on Mespil Road and of Tracton House on St Stephen's Green found new homes in Áras an Uachtaráin and Dublin Castle respectively. Others which were salvaged and reinstated include a very fine example in the foyer of the offices of Sun Alliance on Dawson Street, and two from houses on South Frederick Street in Ballyorney House in Enniskerry. Many less obviously important examples have been lost in all parts of the city, most notably in St Stephen's Green, Parnell Square, Mountjoy Square and Dominick Street.

Many stuccodores made use of existing classical designs as models for their plasterwork, and used prints or engravings as sources. For instance, the ten beautiful classical figures of the muses in the Apollo room at 85 St Stephen's Green (part of Newman House) are very closely modelled on the series of antique statuary by Italian engraver, PA Maffei. The La Francini brothers, who decorated the house in the

Opposite page: The majestic dome of City Hall, constructed in 1769 to the designs of Thomas Cooley. The sense of height is emphasised by the use of coffering, which diminishes in scale as it rises. This domed space was originally used by Dublin's merchants as a place in which to transact business.

Above: A detail of the swags which surround the circular dome windows at City Hall. All of the decorative plasterwork in the dome has recently been repainted and regilded.

early 1740s, simply 'borrowed' the designs and made few, if any alterations. This fact does not detract in any way from their skill in transforming a small, two-dimensional image in a print into a stunning, sensuous figure. The stilted quality of the Italian engravings has been replaced by graceful, drapery-clad figures in a Dublin town house.

An exhibition held in the National Gallery of Ireland in 1991, entitled *Irish Eighteenth-Century Stuccowork and its European Sources*, revealed similar sources for the plasterwork in 9 St Stephen's Green and in the former La Touche Bank in Castle Street (a ceiling now in the Bank of Ireland, College Green), as well as many other notable eighteenth-century houses and public buildings. The charming pair of cherubs who float on the saloon ceiling of 20 Dominick Street were borrowed from an engraving by the noted French painter François Boucher by the house's owner and builder, stuccodore Robert West. Those ceilings have now been meticulously cleaned and restored, and are among some of the most outstanding works of art in Dublin from the Georgian period.

Regency and Nineteenth-Century Plasterwork

Following the Act of Union in 1800, the slump in Ireland's economic prospects was reflected in building practices. Fewer grand houses and housing developments were conceived, though there were exceptions, such as Fitzwilliam Square and Pembroke Road, which were built between 1820 and 1840. In general, plasterwork was confined to cornices, the undersides of staircases and some showy examples in hallways. With the introduction of gas light in the 1820s, houses began to be fitted with central ceiling roses. At that time roses were usually composed of acanthus or vine leaves, or other devices, such as anthemion or honeysuckle motifs. The ceiling rose was generally circular, though ovals and interlocking circles are also to be found. Garlands and wreaths of intertwining bay or oak leaves were very popular in the early 1800s, as was the reeded moulding. Bundles of reeds, sometimes with crisscross straps, were a favourite neo-classical device for ornamenting marble chimney pieces and timber door surrounds, but were also adapted for use in plaster cornices.

The taste for Gothic and Tudor revival became evident in the 1830s, and there are some good examples of Tudor-style ceilings at Old Conna House and Jubilee Hall, both near Bray, and of Jacobean-style ceilings in the library of Airfield House, Dundrum. The plasterwork in the houses of Fitzwilliam Square and Harcourt Terrace is representative of the period between 1820 and 1840. Here honeysuckle motifs, vines and acanthus are used to create broad cornices, but the adherence to strict classical rules has gone. The deep cornices of dentil, rosette and egg-and-dart mouldings are no longer in fashion.

Opposite page
Top: The Jacobean-style ceiling in the library at Airfield House is typical of the 1890s.
Bottom: This ceiling decoration in a narrow hallway in Pearse Street shows how a simple design can be so effective. Such decoration was commonplace in the mid-nineteenth century, even in the humblest houses, in contrast to the plainness of their counterparts in London.

This page
Top: This is an oval ceiling rose, typical of the 1860s and featuring acanthus leaves. Such roses, placed centrally in the ceiling, became the norm following the availability of gas light in Victorian houses. Centrepieces were a rarity in the previous century, when oil lamps and candles were the only source of artificial light.
Bottom: The corner of a ceiling from a large Victorian house, Sharavogue in Glenageary. The use of ivy leaves as a decorative motif is typical of the 1860s.

Woodwork

joinery and carving

The craft of joinery once covered a multitude of skills related to the cutting and working of timber to produce decorative finishes in buildings, including doors, windows, shutters, flooring, staircases, panelling and architraves. It was also linked to the craft of the wood carver or sculptor, and sometimes called for the use of ornamental work. The fitting-out of churches, shops and commercial premises, such as banks, also came within the scope of the joiner.

Even the everyday joinery, like the standard panelled front door, or the typical Victorian staircase with its mahogany handrail, was the product of skilled craftsmanship. In the eighteenth century the guilds controlled their members and apprentices with strict rules. The apprenticeship for a trade in joinery was arduous. An apprentice carpenter or joiner had to master the making of tenons and mitres, dovetail joints, the fitting of locks, the making of drawers, pedestals and counters and the construction of panelled doors, shutters and frames. He had to be able to make something as complex as a splayed circular window, or as robust as a front door.

During the great flowering of architecture in the eighteenth century, the carvers and joiners produced outstanding decorative work, such as the internal doorcases of houses in Henrietta Street, Dominick Street and Parnell Square. These mahogany doors, with their architectural frame of carved architrave and overdoor, are of a quality that ranks with the best in Europe. The woodwork in some

Opposite page: The Billiards room at Gortmore (Gort Muire), Dundrum, a large Victorian building with an elaborate interior, which was remodelled in the 1880s by a wealthy wine merchant named Edward Burke. The house was equipped with extravagant rooms, including a domed conservatory, a smoking room and new staircase and this magnificent Billiards room. It is panelled throughout in oak, with parquet flooring and coved ceilings, and has a splendid tiled fireplace.

of Dublin's churches, such as the carving of the organ case in the Chapel Royal, is outstanding. The box pews and panelling in St Werburgh's, along with the carved pulpit that is supported by the heads of the four evangelists, and the now-vanished carved and gilt reredos of St Mary's Church are magnificent achievements of the Georgian period.

The supply of timber, some of it imported, and the availability of good material from sawmills was also an important factor. At that time, deal was imported from Norway, while expensive mahogany for internal doors came from places as far-flung as Jamaica in the West Indies. Later on a huge quantity of pine was shipped to Ireland from America and Canada.

In the eighteenth century, timberyards that stocked a variety of home-grown and imported woods were generally located along the quays of the River Liffey – especially in the then Port of Dublin – for ease of transport, as can be seen on John Rocque's 1757 map. The impressive arched entrance gate to the Dublin City Sawmills in Thomas Street (now Chadwick's), once owned by Joseph Kelly and Sons, bears testament to the success enjoyed by the timber business in nineteenth-century Dublin. Here, in the 1880s, every kind of joinery work was made to order in their workshops. Not far away, James Fitzsimons of Bridgefoot Street stocked ash, elm, hickory, pine, birch, oak and deal, and also had a wharf and stores at the North Wall. His business was established in 1780 and specialised in roofing timber and slates, and wood for carts and wagons.

Only a handful of seventeenth-century buildings, some of which were discovered only in recent years, survive in Dublin to tell the tale of the joiner's work. The Royal Hospital, Kilmainham, is well documented, and the stairs and internal doors at St Sepulchre's (now Kevin Street Garda Station) have also been recorded in books. However, in recent years, during the threat of demolition, four seventeenth-century houses were discovered in Aungier Street, two on Ormond Quay and another in Smithfield. The house in Smithfield and the one at 29 Ormond Quay have both vanished, but their wooden staircases were saved.

After the seventeenth century, as timber-framed houses and timber construction became outmoded, the role of carpentry developed further into the realm of decorative detail. These details became the work of the joiner. New brick- and stone-built buildings required finely detailed doors, shutters, architraves and other features to bring them to a finished state. However, the carpenter's work also continued to involve the basic tasks of floor- and roof-construction, the laying of floorboards and, in larger and more complex jobs, the erection of scaffolding or shuttering to support masonry and even larger structures, such as domes. For instance, the large dome of the House of Commons, erected in the Parliament House on College Green about 1730, required a series of complicated trusses

Opposite page
Top left and right: A pretty staircase dating from the 1730s in Newcastle House, County Dublin. Craftsmen of the period favoured such fluted balusters with barley-sugar twists. The long, fluted half-column is a baluster from 6 Bachelor's Walk and also dates from the 1730s. At this time all the decorative features of stairs were made of pine and originally would have been painted. Staircases such as these are now a rarity in Dublin as so many houses of the period have disappeared over the past thirty years.
Bottom left: A decorative carved detail from the chapel of the Royal Hospital, Kilmainham, carved by Jacques Tabary, a French Huguenot sculptor.

This page
Above: Decorated panel from the National Museum of Ireland in Kildare Street. It was the work of the Italian woodcarver Carlo Gambi who was brought to Ireland to decorate the woodwork in both the National Museum and the National Library. Gambi's work is a recreation of the Italian Renaissance style with elaborate urns, symmetrical arabesques and scrolls.
Left: A carved capital from a pub- or shopfront in Marlborough Street, dating from the late nineteenth century. The pseudo-Egyptian character of this piece is similar to the capitals of the old Carlton cinema on O'Connell Street.

and beams to support the massive structure.

Carpenters were generally well paid in late eighteenth-century Dublin. An account of alterations carried out to 12 Henrietta Street in 1782 indicates that the carpenters' and joiners' work accounted for £820 out of a total bill for approximately £1,564. Carpenters often earned enough to allow them to become speculative builders in their own right. A successful carpenter might take a lease on one or more building sites and erect a house for himself and perhaps one or two extra buildings, which he would hope to rent or sell.

In general, carpenters, joiners and carvers remain an anonymous group of craftsmen as far as written accounts exist, and their work is rarely signed. There are, however, some exceptions. During the demolition of 14 Parnell Square, an overdoor from the house revealed the signature of John Mack on the reverse, completely hidden from view. The Macks were noted cabinet-makers, located in Abbey Street, who were in the habit of stamping their furniture in this way. A similar find occurred in the 1980s during the demolition of sixteen houses in Eccles Street, when a gesso-decorated staircase bracket was discovered with the following message from its maker: 'For the Lord Mayor's (house), 2 dozen, signed Arthur Mooney.'

The roles of carpenters and joiners became more defined and separate as the joiners concentrated more and more on the visible detail, such as doors, shutters and architraves, while the carpenters laid the joists and produced structural

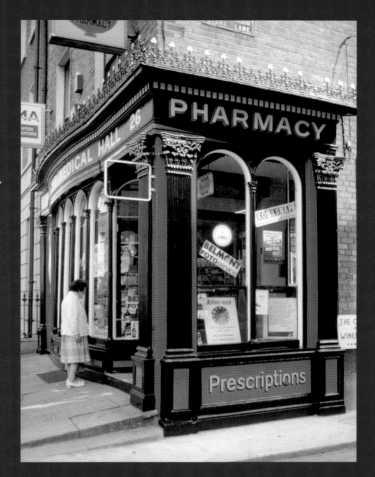

work. The principal rooms and staircases of many early eighteenth-century houses, both large and small, were panelled throughout, which meant that the walls were lined with timber, providing insulation and a pleasing finish. Even the cornices of such rooms, though having the appearance of great solidity, were actually made up of thin pieces of timber. Examples of such work, now quite rare, may be seen in the modest houses of Fownes Street in Temple Bar.

At this time the raised-and-fielded panel was in fashion and, broadly speaking, all doors, shutters and wall panels built between 1720 and 1770 conform to this style. The typical Dublin house of the late seventeenth, or early eighteenth century was a three- or four-storey gable-fronted terraced building, the stairs and main rooms of which were panelled. The house at 25 Eustace Street, restored by the Irish Landmark Trust in the 1990s, is a good example. These gabled houses were known as Dutch Billys because of their similarity to the brick-gabled houses

of Holland. They were once commonplace and quite apparent in early engravings and images of the city, such as Brooking's map of Dublin from 1728. Such houses would have lined the streets of Dublin, and a few examples still exist on Capel Street, Mary Street, the quays, Henrietta Street, St Stephen's Green, Molesworth Street, South Frederick Street and in parts of Temple Bar. The doors and panelling of all these houses were raised and fielded, unlike the simple recessed panels of the late eighteenth and early nineteenth centuries.

In very costly houses, such as those of St Stephen's Green or Henrietta Street, or in larger mansions like Leinster House, the architraves and mouldings about the panels were hand-carved, with mouldings such as egg-and-dart. A fine example is the lavish eighteenth-century doorcase of a house that now forms part of the Merrion Hotel. Equally impressive are the carved overdoors at 20 Dominick Street, which are the work of Richard Cranfield, once the master of the Carpenters' and Carvers' Guild.

The carving in the House of Lords (now part of the Bank of Ireland, College Green), especially of the caryatid figures that ornament the chimney pieces, is of a very high quality indeed. The magnificent panelling, doors and Ionic columns that ornament the lower part of the building's barrel-vaulted entrance and apse are unusual because they are entirely constructed of oak. As was the custom, the oak was left in its natural state but was polished. The natural quality of oak and mahogany was traditionally revealed by oiling or polishing, whereas all pines or inferior woods were painted.

Equally impressive are the carved bookcases in Marsh's Library, constructed in the early 1700s, and those of the Old Library in Trinity College where the galleries of bookcases are supported by fluted Corinthian pilasters and a full classical frieze and cornice, all timber-carved. This exquisite woodwork dates from 1712 to 1730.

There is also high-quality wood carving surviving from an even earlier period, which tells us much about the evolution of the carver's art. The very delicate carving about the east window of the chapel of the Royal Hospital at Kilmainham is among the earliest examples in the country. Its graceful foliate scrollwork and exuberant leaf carving is the work of Jacques Tabary, a French Huguenot sculptor who became a freeman of Dublin in 1682. The quality of Tabary's work and the massive scale of the undertaking is breathtaking. The whole east window surround of the chapel is meticulously articulated by an elaborate composition of fluted columns, scrolls, panels and urns. Tabary must also have carved the semicircular timber panels, or overdoors, which ornament the entrances to the courtyard of the hospital. These are outstanding in composition and subtlety of detail. One is composed of military trophies, while another

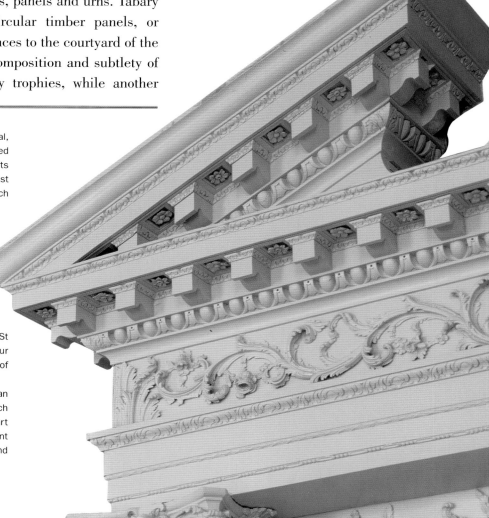

incorporates a crown and the two inverted 'C's of King Charles II.

The National Museum and National Library in Kildare Street display some of the finest nineteenth-century wood carving in the city, although at the time of its execution in the late 1880s complaints were made by Irish cabinet-makers because the carved work was brought over from Italy. Carved doors and chimney pieces were made by Carlo Gambi, a wood carver based in Siena who was brought to Ireland by the architect Thomas Manly Deane. Gambi worked in the Italian neo-Renaissance style, which complemented the design adopted by the Deane practice for both the Museum and the Library. The double-leaved doors, thirty-three in total, were described on the architect's drawings as 'Foreign doors'.

A number of very finely carved chimney pieces were also made for the National Library. The finesse of Gambi's carving is evident in the minute detail of the carved heads, flowers and foliate scrolls which surround the central panel of each door. The panels depict trophies of war, exotic fruits, lion masks, musical and scientific instruments. Arabesques with flowing vine scrolls, vases, urns, birds and grotesque heads are incorporated into the design of the doors. One pair of doors exhibits a fine array of botanical specimens, which reminds us that the building was originally designed as the Museum of Science and Art.

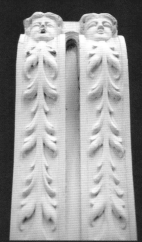

Opposite page: St Mary's Church, Mary Street: part of the elaborate reredos from the east end of the church, behind the altar. This timber screen comprised fluted pillars and an intricately carved frieze and cornice, and was heavily gilded. Unfortunately, the carving can no longer be seen as it was removed in the 1980s.

This page

Above: These two charming brackets, with their cherub heads, are part of a wooden Victorian shopfront in Anglesea Street.

Right: One of a pair of dramatic carved shopfront brackets (*c.*1850) from the frontage of Abrahamson's Tailors in Parliament Street.

Pages 112-113

P112, top left: A pair of late Georgian doors, *c.*1820, at Wilton Place on the Grand Canal. The effect of painting the door, its fanlight and surround in white makes a striking composition against the dark background of the stonework.

P112, middle: A contrasting pair of late nineteenth-century doors in a terrace of brick houses, Charleston Road, illustrates how far the design has departed from the strict classical approach of 100 years earlier. The segmental arched top, and the use of decorative yellow bricks and carved stone details are typical features of terraced houses in Dublin from the 1880s onwards. The concentration of decoration is now applied to the door surround and to the door itself, which is glazed.

P112, bottom left: An unusual and highly detailed Victorian hall door from a house in Appian Way where the door itself is composed of eight raised circular panels. The cut-stone door surround, with its medieval-inspired columns and roll moulding with leaf ornament, indicates the Victorian move away from the classical model and the fact that no expense was spared in the building of the house.

P112, bottom right: One of the many typical eighteenth-century panelled doors from Merrion Square. It was painted in unorthodox bright colours and pictorial panels to celebrate Dublin's millennium.

P113, top right: This door, with its stained-glass panels and brick surround, is typical of the early twentieth-century. Such doors are commonplace throughout Dublin's Victorian into Edwardian suburbs, such as Rathmines, Terenure and Drumcondra.

P113, bottom left: Polished oak doors were frequently used for banks and public buildings in the nineteenth century to create an imposing and sometimes forbidding presence, as in this example from the Bank of Ireland on College Green.

P113, middle right: This large entrance door at Malahide Castle, which is composed of many small panels, is studded with handmade nails in imitation of medieval examples. It dates from the early nineteenth century.

P113, bottom right: While most entrance gates to houses in the nineteenth century were made of cast iron there are occasional examples, such as this at Trinity Hall, Dartry Road, where wood was used. Panels of decorative cast iron were incorporated into the gates, which were supported by substantial hinges.

Doors and Entrances

The typical early eighteenth-century hall door was tall, usually twice the height of its width, and was constructed of six, eight, or even nine panels. Such doors were strongly made, generally using pine, which was painted. At least two larger bolts and a large box-lock provided security on the inside of the door, but safety chains and sometimes iron or wooden bars were used for additional security. A box-lock, with its strong iron mechanism encased in oak and decorated with brass, was usual on such hall doors. Door furniture consisted of a knocker and a knob with which to pull the door shut. Numbers and letter boxes were added much later; the houses in many Georgian streets were not numbered at all and letter boxes were only inserted into doors following the introduction of the Penny Post in 1840. Prior to that, letters were delivered by hand and servants were expected to open the door to receive them.

By the middle of the eighteenth century the proportions of doors had become

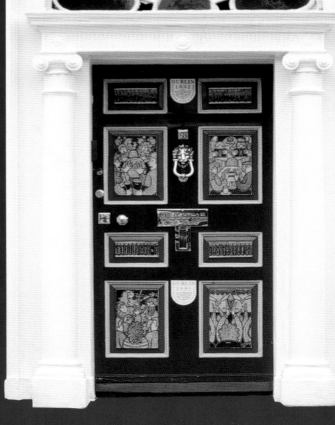

more squat, though raised-and-fielded panelling remained fashionable. Internally, heavy mouldings were common for window and door architraves, while chair rails ran at waist-height around the rooms. The architraves were 'shouldered' or 'lugged' and those about the windows were often supported on sturdy timber pedestals.

Typical mid-eighteenth-century doors had an arrangement of six panels, with four vertical and two horizontal top and bottom panels. By the 1780s these raised-and-fielded panelled doors gave way to plainer and shallower recessed panels. In the early 1800s the Regency taste was for flat panelled doors with delicate mouldings, while architraves and other joinery details also became more refined and delicate.

Late Georgian woodwork was much influenced by the Adam style, leading to the neo-classical taste for refined detail and gesso ornament. Pilasters and overdoors were frequently decorated with gesso, or composition as it was also called, a mixture of plaster and linseed oil that was not unlike putty. Classical details, such as the heads of Roman emperors, urns and scrollwork, were popular devices. Gesso

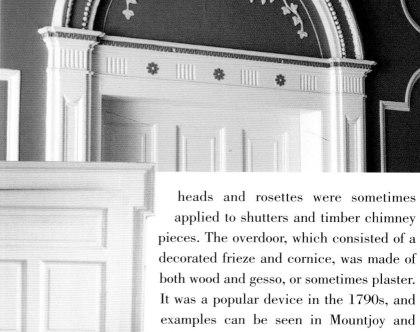

heads and rosettes were sometimes applied to shutters and timber chimney pieces. The overdoor, which consisted of a decorated frieze and cornice, was made of both wood and gesso, or sometimes plaster. It was a popular device in the 1790s, and examples can be seen in Mountjoy and Merrion squares, as well as in large houses in County Dublin.

At this time the fashion for very tall windows, reaching almost from floor to ceiling, took hold and good examples may be seen on Merrion Square, in particular. Shutters began to be placed at a splayed angle to the window, partly to reflect more light into rooms and partly to accommodate the new fashion for hanging curtains instead of the previous festoon curtains, which were hung from the top of the window.

The early nineteenth century saw many new terraced houses being built in places like Fitzwilliam Square, Pembroke Road and Rathmines, still in the Georgian style. Such houses were built for the new middle classes who increasingly wished to live away from the centre of the city. This trend accelerated during the Victorian period, when whole new suburbs were speedily created to the south in Rathmines, Ranelagh, Rathgar and Sandymount, and to the north in

Clontarf, Drumcondra and Glasnevin. New residential towns, such as Kingstown (Dun Laoghaire) emerged and the provision of a good railway service encouraged the creation of Victorian residential districts, such as Monkstown, Dalkey and Killiney.

The doors on these new Victorian houses were typically four-panelled with heavy mouldings that projected out from the frame of the door itself. Front doors sometimes consisted of two tall panels, arched at the top. In public buildings designs varied considerably, with studded, panelled doors appearing on banks, Gothic detailing on churches and elaborate Italian Renaissance treatment on the doors of such impressive structures as the Museum Building in Trinity College. Some of the finest Victorian carving is to be seen on the doors of the National Museum in Kildare Street, produced in the late nineteenth century. Hotels, shops and pubs made use of tall, well-constructed double doors with heavy plate-glass windows. Glass was sometimes etched with lettering, or decorative designs.

Towards the close of the nineteenth century, some front doors incorporated stained-glass panels and sidelights and windows above the door were introduced to admit more light into the hallway. Timber porches also became popular and were a feature of early twentieth-century houses.

Staircases

Seventeenth-century staircases were constructed of oak and were generally robust in character with wide handrails. Two styles of baluster have survived, one a pear-shaped baluster, which can be seen in the Royal Hospital, Kilmainham, and on Aungier Street, and the other with a barley-sugar or twisted design, which has survived at 10 Ormond Quay. Similar barley-sugar-style staircases may also be seen in the Tailors' Hall and in Marsh's Library, both buildings of the early eighteenth century. By the 1720s and 1730s a short baluster comprising a pear-shaped base and a miniature Doric column had evolved and newel posts were formed of paired columns, sometimes Doric, sometimes fluted Corinthian, as was the case at 6 Bachelor's Walk.

The construction of early eighteenth-century stairs included either a straight or ramped handrail, usually of painted pine. As the century progressed the handrail was generally made of mahogany and ended

Below: A carved plaque from one of the bookcases of Marsh's Library, dating from the early eighteenth century.

Bottom right: The mid-eighteenth-century staircase at Loughlinstown House (now the office of the European Foundation). The ramped handrail, which ends in a complex curl at the bottom of the stairs, was a standard feature of the period.

Bottom left: Typical mid-eighteenth-century staircase with its fluted balusters and carved brackets from a house in Parnell Square.

at the bottom in a generous curved scroll. These scrolls, or spirals, of mahogany remained a constant feature of staircases right through the Victorian period.

Throughout the course of the eighteenth century, staircase balusters became progressively thinner and more delicate, sometimes incorporating a small urn into the base. The robust mid-eighteenth-century staircase with its carved wooden brackets or tread-ends gave way to a more refined style with brackets ornamented in gesso pineapples and scrolls of tiny leaves and rosettes. By the late eighteenth century newel posts had vanished, and curved handrails followed the sweep of the stairs, or landing. The slender mahogany handrails were made up in sections, and were sometimes inlaid with boxwood.

The development of staircases in the nineteenth century was characterised by a return to solid, generally less elegant balusters in a wide variety of shapes. Cast-iron balusters were sometimes used instead of timber, and in the late nineteenth century elaborate newel posts, with carved finials and even lamps, made their return.

Top: This early ramped staircase from Marsh's Library in St Patrick's Close gives access to the first-floor rooms. The use of oak and its barley-sugar design are typical features of the early 1700s.
Above right: A curved wood-and-gesso bracket from the staircase of Rosemount, Clonskeagh (now demolished). These brackets or tread-ends were used to ornament the side of each step and were an integral part of the whole staircase design. This slender timber bracket was carefully curved to fit the bend of the staircase, and the delicate gesso ornamentation would have been applied afterwards. Before this type of bracket became common at the end of the eighteenth century, earlier models were hand-carved in local workshops.

Except the Lord build the house they labour in vain that build it ps.cxxvij j.

Lettering

There is so much lettering to be found in Dublin, from all periods and in all styles, that here we can offer only a taste of some of the more interesting examples. The appearance of names and numbers on buildings in the form of signs, inscriptions and dates adds as much to the city's history as to its decoration. The naming of shops, public buildings and streets is an essential requirement to be able to identify places and to find one's way around. But the provision of such lettering also offers great opportunity to signwriters, stone and wood carvers, ironworkers, brass engravers and other craftsmen to display their skills and thereby enhance the visual interest of the streetscape.

One of the earliest surviving street signs in the city is a stone plaque set in the wall at Hume Street, while a cast-iron example in Foster Place is likely to be nearly 200 years old. In the eighteenth century, Latin was frequently used for inscriptions and Roman script on lettering remained the standard choice for stonecutters right through the nineteenth century. The impressive Roman letters carved into the walls of the three locks on the Grand Canal at Ringsend in the 1790s provide a good example of this. Most of the elegant bridges of the Grand and Royal canals also bear stone-carved inscriptions

Above: Lettering and inscriptions have always played an important role on public buildings and on streets, and their use continues to be as valuable today as it ever was. This interesting biblical quotation may seem unusual today in the context of architectural ornamentation, but at the time the message was apt for this building, the YMCA (Young Men's Christian Association) in Rathmines.

Bottom left: From the Malahide Road, this is one of a number of now-rare milestones which once lined the principal routes to the capital. While most of these milestones were made of cut granite, this example is unusual as it is of cast-iron. The character of the lettering and numerals is readily identifiable as early nineteenth-century in style and the lettering is derived from Roman prototypes. Milestones such as this were usually triangular, and had the relevant distance embossed on each face.

Below: The distinctive lettering which forms the fascia of the International Bar on Wicklow Street dates from the turn of nineteenth century. It is also of Roman character, but with a vertical emphasis.

and dates. Mercer's Medical Clinic (formerly Mercer's Hospital) has its name inscribed in large Roman letters on its eighteenth-century façade, and similar well-cut lettering was used on such important civic monuments as Nelson's Pillar in O'Connell Street.

In the mid-nineteenth century, cast-iron plaques that announced and defined the city's electoral wards were erected, and one may be seen, for instance, at the Ship Street entrance to Dublin Castle, indicating the limits of the Royal Exchange Ward. In 1847 the new townships, such as Rathmines, also marked their boundaries with circular plaques of cast iron. One such marker may be seen on Terenure Road East. In Victorian times cast iron was the material of choice to record long inscriptions on commemorative plaques, such as that at the entrance to the People's Park in Dun Laoghaire, or at Victoria Park (now Killiney Hill). Naturally stone was the first choice for inscriptions on important public buildings, such as town halls and courthouses, but as the nineteenth century progressed, iron and terracotta were increasingly used.

The ready availability of terracotta from the 1880s onwards gave rise to a large number of very permanent and decorative name tablets on late Victorian and Edwardian buildings, such as the Iveagh Baths in Bride Road, the YMCA in Rathmines, or the Post Office in Ballsbridge (*see* illustration, p.12). As inscribed terracotta panels had to be hand-modelled and fired in a kiln, such pieces would not have been cheap. Despite this, there are a large number of examples on a wide range of public buildings, such as schools and hospitals, as well as on the gateposts of some private houses.

Engraved brass nameplates have been in use on business premises, churches and other institutions since Victorian times, if not before. A polished brass plate on a hall door has always created an air of distinction or professionalism, and has long been the popular choice for all kinds of business activities.

From the nineteenth century onwards, raised letters made of stucco

Top: A cast-iron logo from the old premises of Kapp and Peterson at the corner of Bachelor's Walk, facing O'Connell Bridge. The use of cast-iron panels such as this to mark a company's location was once quite common.
Above right: An oval plaque, bearing the street name and date, is an unusually attractive example of the stonecutter's craft. Quite a number of Dublin streets once bore such stone name plates, though few now survive.
Right: The inscription over the Iveagh Play Centre, Bull Alley Street, shows the twentieth-century style of lettering, which departs from the previously popular Roman model. This simple style, typical of the early modern movement, has dispensed with the serif, which was a characteristic flourish in Roman script and found at the extremity of each letter.

were popular for hotels, pubs, shops and many other buildings. This inexpensive material was versatile and could be modelled in a variety of styles. The front of the now-vanished Royal Hibernian Hotel in Dawson Street once bore such lettering. The façade of 2 Palace Street was remodelled in the1850s and given a stucco inscription reading: 'The Sick and Indigent Roomkeepers' Society. Founded AD1790.' In the nineteenth century church brasswork, as one might expect, adopted Gothic lettering, and a good example may be seen on the door of the Chapter House in Christ Church Cathedral.

It was shopfronts, however, which offered the signwriter and painter the best opportunity for regular and creative work. Pork butchers, dairies, newsagents – all manner of shops employed the services of the painter and signwriter. Now and again when more recent signs are being removed from buildings, old hand-painted fascia boards with earlier lettering appear beneath. As Dublin does not have many distinguished traditional shopfronts with old lettering, authentic examples should be preserved when they are discovered.

What is known as 'Antique Roman' was once the most popular typeface for lettering, but this was modified into other forms, such as Ornamental Roman, Century Bold, Old Face Heavy and Imprint Shadow. Victorian signwriters made frequent use of Imprint Shadow, as it gave the letters a three-dimensional appearance. In the late Victorian period carved letters on signs were gilded and revealed underneath a background of black-painted glass, producing a strikingly vivid three-dimensional effect.

Ornamental lettering, such as Old English and Ornamental Roman, was often adapted for signs, notices and advertisements. Gothic lettering and 'church text' were popular in the nineteenth century, and Gaelic or Celtic lettering also made its first appearance on the entrance gates of one or two houses. Letters formed in ceramics and wood-carved examples were also once commonplace, but plastic, perspex, steel and neon quickly took over during the last sixty years.

Above: The brass name plate from the entrance to Mitchell's, Kildare Street, was until recent times the most common form of business identification. The variety of design in the lettering, the quality of the brasswork, as well as the actual size and shape of the plates, made this a distinctive feature of Dublin doors in the business districts.
Bottom left: A rectangular, stone street plaque from Highfield Road, Rathgar, dating from the early 1800s. It is built into a brick pier adjoining the railings of a front garden.
Bottom right: Part of a painted shop sign from a newsagent and tobacconist in Stephen Street, demolished recently, is a fine example of the sign-writer's art. Not many traditional hand-painted signs such as this remain to be seen in the city, although sign-writing for new shopfronts is a thriving business.

Top: Lettering (now replaced) at the Fishamble Street entrance to Dublin's Civic Offices is incorporated into the stonework of a low wall.

Above right: An example of modern raised lettering at the entrance to Dublin Zoo, Phoenix Park.

Below right: An example of 1980s illuminated neon lettering from Baggot Cleaners in Baggot Street. In the past sixty years neon has been increasingly used for shopfronts and other signage, having the advantage of being visible at night. Whereas many such signs are lacking in aesthetic quality, the slender tubes employed in this sign produce an attractive result.

Below: An unusual example of old Gaelic script is used here on the gate posts of Carraig-na-Gréine, an early Victorian house in Dalkey. The carefully crafted lettering is carved in granite and utilises a style now almost completely forgotten.

Mantelpieces

Marble mantelpieces, or chimney pieces as they were generally called, have been part of the precious architectural furnishings of houses since the late seventeenth century. Inventories and auction advertisements for houses built in the early eighteenth century show that they were among the most valuable fixtures. They were also among the most desired: there has always been a brisk trade in second-hand marble mantelpieces and people often took their favourite ones with them when they moved house.

Irish eighteenth-century marble mantelpieces were of a very high quality, and there is an extraordinary variety in style, colour and carving. One of the earliest surviving chimney pieces in Dublin is the rare plaster-modelled example from Old Bawn House in Tallaght, dating from 1635 and now installed in the National Museum. This monumental work, which once surrounded a fireplace in the long-vanished archbishop's residence in Tallaght, depicts a biblical scene: the building of the walls of Jerusalem. It is a rare and important remnant from a period for which we have so few examples in the decorative arts, or architecture.

Early eighteenth-century chimney

pieces tended to be constructed of plain slabs of marble, with a simple architrave of egg-and-dart moulding. The opening for the grate was usually square, but balloon shapes and arches were also common. Sometimes, as in the case of the House of Lords in College Green, a carved timber chimney piece surrounded the marble inset. Many plain yet very attractive mantelpieces were made for humbler early eighteenth-century houses in Dublin, often utilising interesting black fossilised marble from Kilkenny. Some of the early eighteenth-century examples bear a rose or shell motif in the centre of the slightly curved crosspiece. Examples may be found in Molesworth Street, Capel Street and Bachelor's Walk.

It was the custom to install impressive stone chimney pieces in the hallways of houses and public buildings, examples of which can be seen in Powerscourt House and Charlemont House. In 1745 the Duke of Leinster constructed the largest, most palatial town house in Dublin: Leinster House on Kildare Street. The house was designed by Richard Castle, a prolific architect who has left a legacy of many beautiful buildings in Dublin and beyond. The rooms were fitted with richly carved marble mantelpieces, many of them made to the design of Isaac Ware and were of the finest quality available at that time. Most were carved in white Carrara marble, with yellow Siena marble for pillars and panels.

A great many different compositions were used in the design of these mantelpieces, but all of them consist of two upright elements, a crosspiece and a shelf. The shelf remained quite narrow until the end of the Georgian period, after which it became both wider and longer. The classical column, so much a feature of the Georgian chimney piece, first began to appear in Irish fireplace surrounds in the late sixteenth or early seventeenth centuries, as at Monkstown Castle, County Cork. Where columns were used, the rules of the classical orders were carefully applied and the mantelshelf projected out in the form of a cornice.

The amount of carving on a chimney piece was reflected in the cost of the finished piece, but most mantelpieces had at the very least a sculpted centre plaque and side cheeks. More elaborate examples, such as those in Leinster House, or in the University Club on St Stephen's Green, were heavily ornamented with carved detail in the form of heads, swags, urns and garlands. Later in the eighteenth century carved plaques featuring classical subjects became the norm. In the Royal Irish Academy of Music on Westland Row, there is a very unusual eighteenth-century chimney piece with elaborate

pointed Gothic features.

An eighteenth-century marble mantelpiece would have cost in the region of £250–£300. It would appear that most were made locally as there were several workshops in Dublin where stonecutters made such chimney pieces. There might have been as many as thirty or forty separate pieces required for the assembly of a mantelpiece of this kind. These individual pieces were stuck together with plaster of Paris, and the whole mantelpiece was fixed to the wall and held in position by strong plaster and ties of brass wire.

A number of very beautiful inlaid mantelpieces exist in Dublin, which are attributed to the Italian craftsman Pietro Bossi. A Bossi mantelpiece consists of decoration in marble paste inlay on a white marble background. A particularly fine example of his work may be seen on the first floor of Charlemont House, now the Municipal Gallery of Modern Art.

The style adopted for mantelpieces in the Regency period was less ornate. Reeded and plain uprights were often used, and little or no carved decoration was applied. The use of coloured marble disappeared and whites and greys predominated. By the 1860s a complete change of style had occurred, and large white marble mantelpieces with arched openings and generously proportioned shelves had become the norm. Later, in the 1880s and 1890s, large timber mantelpieces made of oak and mahogany, and sometimes incorporating an inglenook or seat, were fashionable in houses, shops and offices. Fine examples can be seen at Eason's on Dawson Street, a former insurance office, and in John B's bar in the Gaiety Theatre. This trend for timber mantelpieces was also evident in some Edwardian terraced houses, where painted woodwork complemented decorative tiles.

Opposite page: An example of a high-Victorian drawing room mantelpiece, dating from about 1860. The square opening for the grate has given way to an arch, and the mantelpiece is heavily ornamented with decorative carving.

Above left: An 1890s fireplace from Villiers Road, Rathgar, displays the evolving taste for quirky design features, such as discs, balls and brackets. These, combined with the decorative tiles that flank the grate and its ornate brass hood, are characteristic features of the Victorian and Edwardian house.

Above right: This Georgian mantelpiece presents a strong composition by combining white marble in the brackets and shelf on a background of yellow. These marbles – Carrara white and Siena yellow – are the commonest materials of the Georgian chimney piece. The practice of displaying a mirror over the chimney piece gave emphasis and grandeur to a room.

Murals and Painted Ceilings

Despite the fact that in Dublin there is no strong tradition of decorating interior walls of buildings with mural paintings, there are a significant number of examples to be found. Most painting of the eighteenth and nineteenth centuries consisted of oil paintings, pastels, or watercolours that were framed and could be moved about. The mural, on the other hand, was a permanent fixture.

Probably the largest, most dramatic ceiling paintings in the city are the three large canvases that decorate St Patrick's Hall in Dublin Castle. These paintings, two rectangular and one circular, are the work of the Italian artist Vincenzo Waldré, and were carried out in 1778. The circular painting represents an allegorical vision of Ireland with King George III, while the two flanking rectangular pieces show St Patrick kindling a fire at the Hill of Slane and King Henry II meeting the Irish leaders. Waldré is also credited with having painted the oval ceiling in the former Newcomen's Bank, now the Rates Office of Dublin Corporation, on Cork Hill. This painting, dating to the early 1780s, depicts a scene of plenty, with cherubs and a Greek god floating in a cloud-filled sky.

A major series of murals planned for the ceiling of the chapel of the Rotunda Hospital was, unfortunately, never carried out, owing to the untimely death of Dr Bartholomew Mosse who had commissioned the artist Giovanni Battista Cipriani to carry out a painting of the Nativity. The cancelling of this commission represents a great loss to the decorative history of Dublin.

A good number of the ornate plasterwork ceilings in the eighteenth-century houses of Dublin included painted panels or roundels as part of the overall decorative scheme. Among the best examples of paintings to be found in this form are those at 35 North Great George's Street, at the Royal Irish Academy of Music and at the Dublin Writers' Museum. Also included are the roundels depicting classical figures which once ornamented the drawing-room ceiling of the now-demolished Dominican Convent in Eccles Street. Another noteworthy series is the late eighteenth-century painted panels in Rathfarnham Castle. The drawing-room ceiling of 52 St Stephen's Green has a fine painted centrepiece by Angelica Kauffman, dating from 1771, and the walls of the adjoining music room are decorated with large murals depicting classical figurative groups and musical emblems.

Opposite page
Top: The painted ceiling from the entrance hall of the now-demolished Beaufield House, Stillorgan. The four triangular panels of the ceiling are decorated with musical instruments. Though the house dates from the 1830s, the painted ceilings were probably added in the late Victorian period.
Below left: A detail from the extraordinary wall paintings at Prospect Hall, Goatstown. The murals, which were painted in the early 1800s, depict romantic Italianate landscapes, with

rocky glens and fanciful palaces, and are peopled with soldiers and peasants.
This page
Above right: A series of murals and decorative panels, depicting musical instruments and classical figures, decorate the music and drawing rooms of 52 St Stephen's Green, the eighteenth-century home of David Digges La Touche.
Below: The Victorian painted ceiling of Panter's showroom at 5 Leinster Street.
Below right: A contemporary mural in the Italian style at Newtown House.

In a few rare instances, some houses had the entire wall surface of one or two rooms decorated with murals, the favourite subject being an idealised classical landscape. The drawing room of 49 Merrion Square, now the headquarters of the National University of Ireland, is decorated with romantic Italianate views of wispy trees, rivers and mountains, reminiscent of the style of Claude Lorraine. These murals were painted in about 1830 for Robert Way-Harty who, in 1831, became lord mayor of Dublin. Similar murals were also executed for him in his other house, Prospect Hall in Goatstown. These were rediscovered about twenty years ago after the wallpaper that had been covering them was removed.

In a similar instance, this time at a house in Fitzwilliam Square, the prevailing taste of later times resulted in a remarkable series of early nineteenth-century murals being papered over, only to be rediscovered and restored in 1996 when the house was being refurbished by its present owner, Senator Edward Haughey. Beautiful paintings of classical scenes, Roman charioteers and dancing women were discovered beneath the wallpaper.

Two Victorian buildings associated with the English artist John Hungerford Pollen boast impressive painted decorations. They are the University Church on St Stephen's Green (*see* illustration, p.133) and Clontra House in Shankill, which have paintings in the Byzantine and medieval styles respectively. At Clontra, the ceilings are covered by flocks of birds.

The decorating firms of Thomas Panter and H Sibthorpe & Son were responsible for a large number of painted schemes in houses and other Victorian buildings. Panter's own showrooms at 5 Leinster Street incorporate a ceiling with Italianate painted decoration. The premises is currently being refurbished as part of the National Gallery's Millennium Wing project. A similar decorative scheme was painted by such a firm for the hall ceiling of Beaufield House in Stillorgan, sadly now demolished.

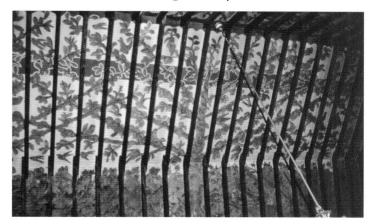

Tiles

Tiles, like most objects of architectural ornament, usually serve some functional purpose alongside their role as decoration. As a ceramic product, they are both heat- and water-resistant and can be easily washed. As a result, they have been used for floors and other surfaces since early times.

The decoration of tiles is a branch of the art of painting, as designs are usually applied with a brush using natural pigments. Medieval tiles, such as those which survive in St Patrick's Cathedral, were often decorated with incised patterns. In other words, the design, or outline, was scratched into the soft clay before the tile was fired in the kiln. Lions, *fleur-de-lis*, trefoils and other geometric patterns were commonly used. Seventeenth- and eighteenth-century Dutch tiles, which occasionally occur in old houses in Dublin, were painted blue or purple with simple designs, usually figurative. Biblical scenes, ships, animals, birds and floral motifs were popular. Their tiles were used to line fireplaces and to cover the walls of dairies and kitchens.

Decorative tiling is often best employed when used as a border to a larger area of plain tiles. Tile painters developed borders and friezes by taking inspiration from classical themes, such as the Greek Key pattern, or vine scroll. During the nineteenth century the tile industry blossomed and an unending assortment of designs was made available for use in houses – as floors in porches, as hearths for fireplaces, and in bathrooms. In public buildings tiles were widely used, particularly in churches, hospitals and offices, such as banks. Shops, especially butchers' shops, used them for walls, floors and even on shopfronts.

Opposite page: A typical Victorian fireplace tile.

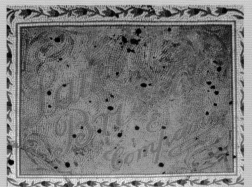

Encaustic floor tiles were made by stamping the thick clay with a die, leaving a pattern that would then be filled with coloured liquid clays. Such tiles were very popular in churches from the 1860s onwards.

The ambitious restoration of Christ Church Cathedral in 1875 included the laying of a magnificent new tiled floor in which original medieval examples were reproduced. The taste for medieval, or Gothic designs was enthusiastically advocated at this time by the architect Augustus Welby Pugin and by the writer John Ruskin, and lavishly decorated churches, such as SS Augustine and John's in Thomas Street, were the result.

Many new designs were exhibited in the Great Exhibition in Dublin in 1853, where the virtues of mass-production and industrialisation were extolled. William Morris, the great designer and leader of an artistic revolt, opposed the principals of mass-produced ornament, and his business, Morris, Marshall, Faulkner and Company, produced many excellent tile designs of its own. Morris, a designer of tapestries, rugs, wallpaper and many other objects, developed a whole range of tiles, including his well-known 'Daisy Tile', 'Tulip and Trellis' and 'Four Pink and Hawthorn' tiles, which date from the 1870s and 1880s.

Decorative tile-making does not appear to have been carried on in nineteenth-century Ireland, perhaps because of the huge selection available from England at modest cost. Tiles were also relatively easy to transport. The major manufacturers, such as Maw and Company, were based in the Ironbridge region at Jackfield in Shropshire, where high-quality clay and cheap coal were both available. Quarry tiles, or floor tiles were produced in Ireland by brickworks, but they tended to be of the coarse quality used in kitchens and basements.

The tiled porch became a standard feature of late Victorian and Edwardian

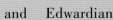

terraced houses and Dublin's suburbs, such as Terenure and Glasnevin, abound with examples of such work, from the relatively plain red, buff and black paving to highly ornamental compositions incorporating triangles, squares, lozenges with *fleur-de-lis*, sunflowers and many other devices.

The Victorian fireplace provided another opportunity for the tile-manufacturer, as tiles were used both to pave the hearth and to line the sides of a cast-iron grate. The earlier preference for a slab of marble, or slate to serve as the hearthstone gave way, from the 1880s onwards, to rich displays of coloured tiles. English makers, such as Maw and Company, and Minton, specialised in heavy tiles that were usually about three-quarters-of-an-inch thick (19mm) and could withstand the heat and general wear-and-tear associated with the fireplace. The side panels of Victorian fire grates gave great scope to the producers of tiles. A standard number of tiles, usually five, was sometimes used to create a single 'picture', or decoration. Historical scenes, representations of the arts, floral motifs, birds, geometric patterns, and sometimes just plain tiles were all available.

By the late nineteenth century there was an insatiable demand for decorative tiles, especially from house-builders. Within thirty years Maw and Company, founded in 1850, had become the largest decorative tile factory in the world.

While the Victorians adapted many 'realistic' subjects, such as flowers, birds and people, for their designs, culminating in highly representational images, the designs of the Art Nouveau era in the early 1900s incorporated stylised, quite abstract patterns and motifs. Strange plants with tall stems and elongated flowers, such as tulips, were popular. A palette of odd pinks, acid greens and maritime blues became fashionable.

Top: The front of Bewley's Café in Grafton Street makes use of mosaic in its Art Deco design.

Above: Marble mosaic and tiles are used in the richly colourful interior of the University Church, St Stephen's Green.

Wallpaper

The fashion for decorating rooms with wallpaper had developed widely in Dublin by the mid-eighteenth century. Many quite modest town houses displayed attractive wallpapers, and this means of interior decoration remained popular right up until the middle of the twentieth century. The oldest-known example of wallpaper in Ireland is a small piece that was found on the back of a door at the Royal Hospital, Kilmainham. It is thought to date to the end of the seventeenth century, and is simply painted and overprinted with a flock design. The flock, made of tufts of fabric like wool, gave the designs a sort of fuzzy, raised texture. Another example of an intact decoration with flock wallpaper is to be seen in the drawing room at Newbridge House in Donabate, North County Dublin.

Most eighteenth-century papers were hand-printed in lengths of about six, or nine feet (1.8m, or 2.7m). Some of the earliest wallpapers were imported from China and were in vogue elsewhere in Europe. Unfortunately, very few examples of papered rooms survive anywhere in Dublin, though an example of Chinese style does exist, again at Newbridge House. Here in the museum, colour pictures representing scenes from Chinese life, including scenery, buildings, boats, rivers and figures, are framed by patterns of imitation bamboo.

Panels of eighteenth-century Chinese wallpaper also once decorated Lord Cloncurry's seaside house, Maretimo, in Blackrock.

Over the last thirty years, an interesting selection of fragments of old wallpaper has come to light during refurbishment work on buildings, indicating that Dublin's rooms were once papered with very lively and quite colourful patterns. Plants, foliage, flowers and birds have always featured in wallpaper, although classical motifs, including swags, garlands and arabesques, occur frequently too. Strong blues and reds with bold, dark patterns were also commonplace. Philip Hussey's well-known painting (*An interior with members of a family*, 1750: National Gallery of Ireland), portraying a family posing in the first-floor front room of their house, shows the walls of the drawing room decorated with then-fashionable 'pillar-and-arch' wallpaper, a classically inspired design printed in a greyish hue.

At that time, wallpaper would have been made and hung by tradesmen known as paper-stainers, and various newspaper advertisements and records from street directories show that there was no shortage of paper-stainers in Dublin during the eighteenth and nineteenth centuries.

Throughout the eighteenth century there was a tax on the manufacture and sale of wallpapers in England, but this apparently did not come into force in Ireland until an Act of 1797. After this time, all wallpapers had to be stamped to show that the levy had been paid. The Victorian period heralded a great change in wallpaper production, as paper became available in rolls and the printing process became mechanised. Designs were mass-produced and the use of wallpaper was universal, especially in the late nineteenth century.

Opposite page: A section of Regency wallpaper was discovered in the Record Tower at Dublin Castle, beneath the early nineteenth-century bookshelves.
This page
Top: This example of Anaglypta wallpaper, or frieze, similar to that in the Dublin Writers' Museum on Parnell Square, was discovered in a dump.
Above: A Chinese-style wallpaper dating from the eighteenth century once decorated the wall of Maretimo in Blackrock.

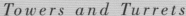

A city without towers, spires, domes, or cupolas would present a dull prospect. The vertical emphasis provided by such architectural features gives welcome variety to the city's skyline and creates landmarks in the often monotonous landscape of its modern surroundings. For instance, the long vista of Rathmines Road is given a focal point by the 128-feet-high (39m) clock-tower of the Town Hall, erected there in 1895. Similarly, the Italianate tower of Dun Laoghaire Town Hall, dating from the 1880s, is a prominent feature of the town and harbour. The townscape is undoubtedly enhanced by such landmarks.

Though towers seem to have proliferated in the Victorian age, gracing many public buildings, such as railway stations, town halls, fire stations, schools and colleges, as well as private houses, they were, of course, an important feature of the classical tradition, too. Many of Dublin's best-known eighteenth-century public buildings, such as Dr Steevens's Hospital, Dublin Castle, or the Rotunda Hospital, have noble examples. While an early type may be seen at the Royal Hospital, Kilmainham.

A surprising number of detached houses of the eighteenth and nineteenth centuries were built with towers, or had lookouts, or turrets added at a later date. The lofty water tower built in the 1870s on the Guinness estate at Farmleigh, Castleknock, doubles as a clock tower. It stands overlooking the Liffey valley at Palmerstown and is constructed of limestone and granite. Likewise, a fine tower still stands at St Anne's in Raheny, in the grounds of another Guinness house, while not far off, on the Malahide Road, there is an ornate example at the house that now forms the centrepiece of Mount Temple School. Many people classify this kind of tower as some sort of folly – a useless structure built at the whim of a rich owner. However, such towers did serve a purpose, for example, to display a clock, as a lookout, to provide ventilation, or to house a water tank, or indeed to act as both clock tower and water tower simultaneously.

The belvedere (*bel-vedere*, beautiful to see) on the roof at Woodlands in Santry, an early eighteenth-century house, was designed as part of the overall symmetrical composition, one where chimneys and windows were all in harmony. It provided a fine view of the surrounding countryside in Clonshaugh. Elsewhere, at Shanganagh Castle near Bray, a circular tower incorporating mock battlements was part of an elaborate early nineteenth-century refurbishment of an older, plainer house in an attempt to gothicise and romanticise its appearance. It also

Opposite page

Top left: The Farmleigh clock tower, Castleknock, is about 200-feet high (61m), and is surmounted by an iron weathercock. The clock, sporting a dial thirteen feet in diameter (4m), was made by the noted Dublin clock-maker, Howard Grubb. It has recently been restored as part of the Government's restoration of the whole estate and house. After a long silence, the bells now chime once more.

Bottom left: The Victorian timber belfry with its attractive slated roof at the Convent of Mercy, Booterstown Avenue. While the eighteenth century provided the city with notable landmarks in the shape of domes, towers and cupolas, the nineteenth century contributed a large number of church spires, which punctuate the skyline.

This page

Right: The attractive octagonal cupola of the Iveagh Play Centre, now the Liberties College, in Bull Alley Street, which was built in 1915.

Below: An open cupola and weathervane crowns the pediment of the former Grand Canal Hotel at Portobello (now Portobello House). This building, one of a chain of five Grand Canal hotels, was built along the route to the River Shannon and was erected in 1807.

Bottom right: A mock medieval tower with Gothic doors and windows was built in 1810 as a folly in the grounds of Glendruid House, near Cabinteely.

afforded a fine sea view. A similar octagonal tower was added to Glenageary House in about 1840 with the idea of providing views of the surrounding Dun Laoghaire coastline, then quite rural and undeveloped. The entrepreneur William Dargan had the same intention when he rebuilt Mount Anville in 1849 and added a spacious viewing tower.

Towers and cupolas, both large and small, were frequently incorporated into the designs of nineteenth-century institutional buildings, such as the Masonic Girls' School at Ballsbridge, now Bewley's Hotel. Two institutional homes for the elderly, the Mageough Home in Rathmines and the Shiels Residence in Stillorgan, display their Victorian credentials with attractive towers. The Mageough Home, laid out on three sides of a square, was built in 1878, while the Shiels Residence, also planned around an internal courtyard, was erected in 1869. Its tower is bedecked with carved dragons.

In the city, Amiens Street Railway Station, now Connolly Station, was equipped with a pair of Italianate towers when it was built in the mid-1840s. An exotic feature of College Green's impressive array of banks is the circular tower of the former Royal Bank, built in red sandstone and capped with a conical roof. It was designed in 1893 by WH Lynn in the style of a hybrid French château. Similarly, in 1894 the Liverpool and Lancashire Insurance Company erected a miniature Gothic château at the corner of Westmoreland and D'Olier Streets, overlooking O'Connell Bridge. Built of stone with a Gothic turret, it is typical of the late Victorian love of historicism and fantasy.

One of Dublin's finest examples is the red-brick Italianate lookout tower at Tara Street Fire Station, erected in 1900 to the designs of the city architect, CJ McCarthy. It is modelled on the medieval towers of Italian hill towns, like those in Siena and Orvieto. Another delightful tower with a conical, slated roof forms part of the present Permanent TSB building in Rathmines, originally erected in 1901 for the Belfast Banking Company.

Though domes cannot really be classified along with towers and cupolas, they too make a striking addition to the skyline of the city. Among the first eighteenth-century domes are, of course, the City Hall, the Four Courts and the Custom House, while we must also include the Church of Our Lady of Refuge in Rathmines and Penney's in Mary Street as imposing Victorian examples.

Opposite page

Top left: The majestic Baroque-style dome and cupola of Penney's in Mary Street was originally erected in 1902 for the department store Todd Burns. The date appears in the copper weathervane above the cupola.

Top right: An unusual cupola surmounting the former Baggot Street Hospital has a small balustrade. The ornate building was built in 1892 and was inspired by the Flemish Renaissance architecture of Brussels and Antwerp.

Bottom left: One of several corner buildings on O'Connell Street, built in the 1920s, which are distinguished by their stonework and cupolas.

This page

Top right: The façade and cupola of Dr Steevens's Hospital, designed by Thomas Burgh, dates from 1720 to 1733. The clock was installed in 1735 in the attractive octagonal cupola.

Bottom right: The dome of Government Buildings creates a dramatic feature on Merrion Street. The main section of the building, with its distinctive lead-covered dome and cupola, was erected in 1911 as the College of Science.

Page 140

Top left: A public clock at Clery's, erected within the last twenty years, has become a landmark of the famous department store whose origins date back to 1853.

Middle left: One of the very few examples of sundials in Dublin is this stone-carved one at the Royal Hospital, Kilmainham, erected in 1680.

Bottom: The three-sided projecting clock at Findlater's on George's Street, Dun Laoghaire, was once a well-known feature of the town. It probably dates from about 1901 when the premises was rebuilt.

Page 141

Top left: The clock on the west front of the King's Inns, with its elegant stone

surround. The roundel draped with a garland was a favourite decorative motif of James Gandon, who designed the building in 1795.

Top right: Dating from 1815, this clock is situated on the south front of the Church of SS Michael and John at Essex Street. The clock is framed in the Gothic style with a stone quatrefoil.

Bottom right: This distinctive building with its clock was erected in the 1920s as the new offices of the Dartry Dye Works in Milltown.

Public Clocks

The importance of clocks, bells and other methods of timekeeping has been recognised for centuries, and it has often been noted that the Irish word *clog* means both bell and clock. Privately owned clocks or timepieces were rare until the eighteenth century, and even then only the rich could afford them. Public clocks, however, are recorded in Dublin as early as the sixteenth century. The oldest working public clock in the city is that of Dr Steevens's Hospital, installed in 1735 and still wound by hand.

There are a good many turret clocks of this type, such as those at the former Mercer's Hospital, or at Tara Street Fire Station, and most of them were made in Dublin. The clock tower of Mercer's Hospital was cleverly positioned at the junction of two buildings, closing the view from South William and South King streets. The clock dial, with gold letters against a blue face, is framed by a circle of stone and has a pediment supported on brackets.

Other clock types included wall-mounted clocks, such as that at Trinity College, and projecting clocks, like the well-known ones at Eason's and Clery's on O'Connell Street. The *Irish Times* clock on D'Olier Street is another good example of a projecting clock, as it is mounted on elaborate

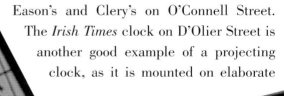

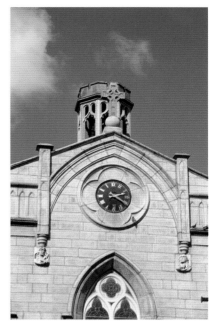

wrought-iron brackets with a skeletal dial and a glass face. Some of the best-known triangular projecting clocks, such as that of Findlater's in Rathmines, have vanished, but others survive on public houses, like Bowes, Bruxelles and the Parnell Mooney. Findlater's, a noted Family Grocers, Wine and Tea Merchants established in Dublin in 1823, had several handsome premises, including Dun Laoghaire, Dalkey, Blackrock, Rathmines, Howth and Baggot Street, and each had a fine public clock.

Most of the clocks were produced locally to a very high standard. The Abbey Presbyterian Church clock was made by Jameson of Grafton Street in 1864, while the firm of J Booth and Sons made clocks for Trinity College, the Royal College of Surgeons, Guinness and the old Ballast Office at O'Connell Bridge. In 1854 Booth also made the fine clock for the tower at St Anne's, Raheny (*see* illustration, p.15). The Mercer's Hospital clock was made in 1907 by Ganter Brothers of South Great George's Street. Dobbyn's of Wicklow Street produced a number of beautiful internal clocks for premises like the former Allied Irish Bank in College Street, the National Library and the Bank of Ireland in College Green.

The dials of most public clocks were traditionally painted black, or dark blue with gold numerals. The most distinctive type are the black-and-gold examples, such as those at St Patrick's Cathedral, Dublin Castle and at the Custom House. The present clock in St Patrick's Cathedral, which was made in England, was installed in 1864 during the refurbishment of the building. It is a very impressive piece, with each dial stretching eight feet (2.4m) in diameter.

Weathervanes

Weathervanes, or weathercocks as they are often called, have been popular decorative devices for the tops of spires and towers since medieval times. The purpose of the weathervane is to tell the direction of the wind, and in the days before weather forecasts and satellite pictures this information was useful to seafarers, farmers and the general populace.

Most weathervanes and finials were made of wrought iron, though copper was used for the moving parts. Though such ironwork offered the blacksmith considerable scope for originality, the cock was the most commonly used motif, to the extent that the term 'weathercock' is more familiar than 'weathervane'. This is attributed to the fact that in the sixth century Pope Gregory the Great declared the cock to be a symbol of Christianity, as an

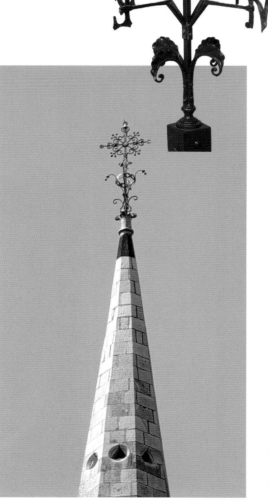

emblem of watchfulness. Following this pronouncement, the cock was deemed the most suitable symbol for church buildings and was subsequently widely used. Sometimes the cock is positioned atop a cross that in turn rests on a globe, symbolising the power of the Church all over the world. Other images were employed too, however, such as the fish, ship, horse, or even a saint. A fine galloping horse makes a striking example at the RDS show-jumping grounds.

The majority of the weathervanes decorating Dublin's church spires, cupolas and towers date from the nineteenth century, either because they were replaced at that time, or because there was greater opportunity for such ornament in the Victorian period. Most weathercocks were large structures, up to eight-feet (2.4m) tall, because they were designed to be seen from far below. Also, in order to turn effectively in the wind the cock, fish, or whatever bird was represented needed an exaggeratedly large tail that would catch the slightest breeze. A good example is the modern peacock weathervane that graces the clock tower on the Chester Beatty Library in Dublin Castle. It was made in the 1990s to the design of Rachel Joynt, and is an appealing addition to the decorative features of the castle.

Monograms, family initials, or dates were also sometimes incorporated into weathervanes, as in the example shown here from a Victorian house in Killiney.

Outdoor Stucco

The fashion for decorating the exteriors of buildings with a hard plaster, or stucco, took root in the early nineteenth century. Stucco, which was a type of render or cement, was composed of burnt limestone, sand and plaster, plus other additives, such as burnt clay or brick dust, which would make it very hard. It was versatile and could be used to run architraves, string courses and pediments, in fact, almost any architectural ornament. The hard reddish-coloured plaster or stucco was sometimes called Roman cement, and lent itself to casting and copying the ornament of other periods. Urns, lions and eagles were popular for the parapets of houses, porches and arched entrances to yards. New terraced houses could be rendered, or stuccoed, and painted in imitation of stone, but at a fraction of the cost of stonework. Such stucco was generally painted, although this was not always the case. Aside from aesthetic considerations, the effects of regular painting helped to preserve the stuccowork.

Alongside widespread use of stucco for house-building, the builders of pubs, hotels and shops were also quick to see its advantages. For example, much of the elegant façade of the Shelbourne Hotel, erected in 1865, relies on stucco for its richly decorative effect. Most of Dublin's nineteenth-century hotels were comprised of two or more old Georgian houses, and their architects made clever use of the economical option presented by stucco to create a unified façade by adding harmonising architraves, string courses and parapets. The Royal Hibernian Hotel in Dawson Street and the Four Courts Hotel on the quays were good examples.

Harcourt Terrace, Dublin's earliest symmetrical group of houses comprised of a grand centrepiece and portico, was built by 1840 and was one of the first terraces to sport façades finished in stucco. The Regency-style architecture of the terrace is characterised by low flanking wings, which connect the pairs of houses, and stucco detailing, such as the architraves around the windows. De Vesci Terrace in Dun Laoghaire, completed in 1843, is not dissimilar in style and is typical of the Victorian coastal architecture of Monkstown, Dun Laoghaire and Clontarf.

From the nineteenth century onwards, many pubs and shops erected

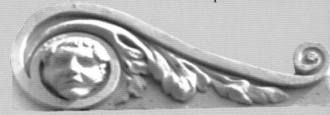

elaborate stucco façades and in two cases remarkable use was made of it to celebrate the cause of Irish nationalism. The Oarsman pub in Ringsend is decorated with a stucco panel depicting a round tower, harp and Irish wolfhound, while the long-vanished Irish House pub at Wood Quay, erected in 1870, once displayed life-size figures of Henry Grattan and Daniel O'Connell, alongside a figure of *Erin* weeping over a stringless harp. When the building was demolished in 1956, all of the stuccowork, including wolfhounds and round towers, was salvaged and now awaits a suitable new home.

Slattery's public house in Capel Street is a striking example of a Victorian stucco-fronted pub, though some of its more extravagant detail has been removed. Many business premises made use of stuccowork to embellish their premises and advertise their wares. For instance, the Vestment Ware Rooms in Parliament Street had an elaborate first-floor sign in stucco, while not far off Lipton's at the corner of Dame Street and Eustace Street displayed a large bowl of plaster fruits to symbolise its grocery business.

By far the greatest use of stucco was its application on Victorian houses, which in some areas, like Dun Laoghaire, Monkstown and Malahide, were universally plastered. Houses both large and small were ornamented

This page

Top left: Sharavogue in Glenageary is a substantial Victorian house (*c.*1870) with a grandiose double staircase and porch, ornamented in the Italianate style, using stucco.
Above right: A decorative stucco panel from a bay window of the Parliament Hotel on Lord Edward Street. This neo-Renaissance stucco ornament dates from the 1880s and formerly decorated a Dublin Corporation office.

Opposite page

Top right: This framed oval plaque, made of stucco, has long served as an advertisement panel on the wall of a building in Temple Lane.
Bottom left: Ornamental stucco, carved wood and cast iron are part of the ornate porch and entrance to the Olympia Theatre on Dame Street, which dates from the late 1890s.
Middle right: A plaster representation of Daniel O'Connell from the long-vanished Irish House pub on Wood Quay. When it was built in 1870, it was regarded as an 'unsightly structure' by architectural commentators.
Bottom right: Eagles made from Roman cement or stucco were popular ornaments for the parapets of houses throughout the first half of the nineteenth century.

with stucco cornices and balustrades, along with architraves and pediments for the windows and doors. Porches, gate lodges, gate piers and entrances to stables or coach-houses were all candidates for this kind of Italianate stucco architecture. Dun Laoghaire's three principal yacht clubs – the Royal Irish, the Royal St George and the National – all built in the Victorian period, were distinguished by their design and stucco detailing.

As with any popular trend, stuccowork did not meet with universal approval. Some nineteenth-century architectural observers were not impressed by it and referred to houses decorated in this manner as 'gimcrack'. However, most of these buildings have endured the Irish climate remarkably well and are still in sound condition.

Coats of Arms

The decoration of buildings with coats of arms is a long-discontinued practice that now seems archaic and old-fashioned. In the past, however, it was an important symbol of the prestige and status of the occupier – whether private or public. Coats of arms appeared on guildhalls, court houses, markets, the office of Dublin Corporation and on buildings erected by the government, such as Parliament House and Custom House. Some institutions, such as the RDS and the Masonic Order, and wealthy owners of private houses employed stonecutters to carve their arms.

Among the many examples of family coats of arms that can be seen on private houses, mainly in County Dublin, are those of the Bruce family at Rockfort Manor on Stradbrook Road, Blackrock, which comprise an elaborate escutcheon and the motto: 'Do well, doubt not.' This piece dates from the 1880s and is medieval in character, which suits the Tudor-revival architecture of the house. At Aldborough House, near the Five Lamps, an earlier, more classical example may be seen in the pediment where two figures flank a shield. This is the arms of the Earl of Aldborough, who built this mansion as his town house in the 1790s.

The language of heraldry is complex and must be correctly contrived. The right to display a coat of arms was granted by the Ulster King of Arms from his offices in Dublin Castle. The granting of a Royal warrant by the monarch allowed an organisation or business to display the Royal Arms on their premises and to incorporate it into their own emblem. At the Royal Hospital in Kilmainham, for instance, a beautifully carved shield surrounded by rich foliage, a lion mask and a crown displays the Royal motto: *Honi soit qui mal*

y pense. The Victorian Royal Arms of the Bakers' Guild that once decorated their building in Bridge Street, and which is now stored in the National Museum, is probably the only example now surviving from a Dublin guild.

The eighteenth-century Arms of Ireland are represented in the magnificent carvings by Edward Smyth on the Custom House, with the Lion and the Unicorn supporting an Irish harp surmounted by a crown. This emblem reveals the delicate political balance in eighteenth-century Ireland between Irish independence and loyalty to the Crown. An elegant oval escutcheon, carved in stone over the main entrance to the RDS in Ballsbridge, shows a figure of Minerva or *Hibernia* seated with her harp and two flowing cornucopias, but no Royal Arms. It dates from the early 1900s when the Society's new premises were built.

Opposite page

Top: Three variants of the Dublin City coat of arms, all showing the three castles burning, which is said to represent the zeal of the citizens to defend the city. Two figures bearing palms or laurel boughs flank the shield. *Top left* is a cement or stucco example from a structure in Merrion Square; *top right* is from the City Assembly House (now Civic Museum) in South William Street; and *middle left* is from the ironwork porch of the Mansion House, as it shows the lord mayor's mace and the civic sword.

Bottom left: The coat of arms of the Calvert Stronge family appears in a lozenge-shaped panel on the wall of the house at Mount Temple School. The Dutch-gabled house was built by the Calvert Stronges in 1862 and has an elaborate clock tower.

Bottom right: A Royal coat of arms, carved in stone in 1901, from the entrance to the Royal Victoria Eye and Ear Hospital on Adelaide Road.

This page

Top left: The coat of arms of the Earl of Aldborough, carved in stone between 1792 and 1798, on the pediment of Aldborough House at the Five Lamps.

Top right: This Dublin City coat of arms carved in red sandstone on the former Grafton Cinema in Grafton Street dates from the late Victorian period.

Middle: An elegantly carved emblem of the RDS decorates the main entrance to their Ballsbridge premises.

Bottom: The coat of arms over the main door to St Patrick's Hospital, Bow Lane, begun in 1749 with funds bequeathed by Dean Jonathan Swift.

Statuary

In the 1740s the Royal Dublin Society established a school for painting and sculpture, the Dublin Society Schools, which was the predecessor of today's National College of Art and Design (NCAD). The celebrated sculptor John van Nost, who had come to Ireland from England in about 1749, taught there, training his pupils in the classical style. From that time on, Dublin began to produce its own sculptors and artists, although there was always input from abroad as well. As a result, the eighteenth century marked a high point in the carving of architectural statuary in Ireland. Dublin's most noted public buildings of the period were all embellished by the work of leading sculptors, such as John van Nost, Simon Vierpyl and Edward Smyth. Two of the city's most striking statues, carved by van Nost in 1753, are the figures of *Mars* and *Justice* that surmount the imposing gates in the Upper Yard of Dublin Castle. A most prolific sculptor, van Nost was responsible for many church monuments and for a statue of King George III that once stood at the Royal Exchange (now City Hall).

The remarkable sculptural detail that ornaments the Casino at Marino was chiefly carried out by Simon Vierpyl, another English sculptor, who settled in Ireland in about 1756. In fact, his decision to move to Ireland was in large part due to the builder and owner of the Casino, Lord Charlemont. He had met Vierpyl in Rome and enticed him to come to Ireland by commissioning him to undertake work on the Casino. Having studied Roman sculpture and statuary at first hand, Vierpyl combined this knowledge with his superb skill to produce, for example, the exquisite urns at the Casino and the refined stone carving that decorated the Royal Exchange.

Edward Smyth, who was born in County Meath, was a pupil of Vierpyl at the Dublin Society Schools. He put his great sculptural skills

Opposite page

Top left: A rare example of medieval stone carving in Dublin is this tomb in St Werburgh's Church. The sculpted fifteenth-century tomb and double effigy is said to be that of Thomas, the seventh-century Earl of Kildare and his wife.

Bottom left:

The statue of *Mars*, spear in hand with a lion at his feet, stands confidently guarding the left-hand arched entrance in Dublin Castle's Upper Yard. It was carved in lead by John van Nost.

Bottom right: This impressive composition was carved by James Pearse and Edward Sharpe for the National Bank in College Green, which was founded by Daniel O'Connell.

This page

Top: The head of Brian Boru is one of the dozens of masterful sculptures which ornament the Chapel Royal (*c.*1807) in Dublin Castle.

The carving is principally the work of Edward Smyth.

Bottom left: The statue of *Justice*, gracefully holding aloft her scales and sword, stands over the Cork Hill gate to Dublin Castle. Also carved in lead by van Nost, it has been the subject of many quips: 'Justice has her back turned on the people of Ireland' and 'Justice rains through the holes in her scales'.

Page 152-153

Three of these photographs show details of the sculpture in the pediment of the Custom House, carved by Edward Smyth. *Top (p.152)*, the representation of a pair of sailing ships of the type which would have been a common sight in eighteenth-century Dublin; *Middle left (p.152)*, the exuberant head of Neptune, god of the sea; and *bottom right (p.153)*, the centrepiece is composed of the figures of *Neptune*, *Britannia* and *Hibernia* with her Irish harp.

Bottom left: 'A Statue that Never Was': A most convincing fibreglass and plaster equestrian statue of Queen Victoria was erected in Dame Street in the 1990s as part of the filmset for *Michael Collins*.

Bottom right: One of a series of four Nubian statues that support lamps in the form of torches outside the Shelbourne Hotel. Two are modelled as princesses and two are slave girls.

Page 153, Top: A cast-lead head of the archangel Gabriel from St Michael's Church, Dun Laoghaire. The late nineteenth-century church was destroyed by fire in 1966.

to use on the buildings of James Gandon, most notably the Custom House. Smyth's lively style was well suited to a classical building as large as the Custom House, a fact best appreciated in the sculpted keystones, or when seeing his work in silhouette on the roofline. Smyth's sculptural composition over the main entrance to the Custom House is less frequently commented on, perhaps because it is more difficult to see. Here the pediment contains the figures of *Hibernia*, *Britannia* and *Neptune*, and was supposed to represent the friendly trading relations between Britain and Ireland. However, the facial expressions of the two ladies do not suggest that they were very happy together!

Several important public statues were created in the early nineteenth century, including that of Admiral Nelson for the pillar, which was blown up in 1966. The admiral's massive head (surviving in the Civic Museum) is an indication of the huge scale of the original figure. It was carved in 1809 by Thomas Kirk, a sculptor who had also received his training in the Dublin Society Schools. John Henry Foley, who modelled the figures for the O'Connell Monument in about 1870, also produced the well-known and striking statues of Oliver Goldsmith (1861), Edmund Burke (1868) and Henry Grattan (1876), which stand in College Green.

As we have already seen, the craft of stone carving and the art of sculpture continued to flourish throughout the nineteenth century, especially with the many new churches, banks and other stone buildings that were being constructed at the time. The work of the O'Shea Brothers on the Museum Building in Trinity College has already been noted.

The firm of stonecutters CW Harrison, established in 1862, had showrooms and workshops on Pearse Street and produced much high-quality architectural stonework, including that of the Kildare Street Club, the Fruit and Vegetable Markets at St Mary's Lane and many of the Victorian banks and insurance company offices on Dame Street. Harrison himself was particularly good at the small detail required for carving plants and animals. His clever and beautifully carved monkeys, which are seen playing billiards about the base of the columns on the Kildare Street Club (*see* illustration, p.78) are legendary. It was said that Harrison was such a perfectionist he would inspect carving in his workshop with a magnifying glass.

James Pearse, the father of 1916 revolutionary Padraig Pearse, was another distinguished stone carver and sculptor. He too had his workshop on Pearse Street. Pearse, who had converted to Catholicism in 1870, won many contracts for church work, such as the statuary on the spire of SS Augustine and John's Church on Thomas Street.

Both James Pearse and his colleague, Edmund Sharpe, had trained in Harrison's before going out on their own, and they were responsible for such outstanding work as the figure of *Hibernia* that stands over the Bank of Ireland building in College Green. Sharpe, who was originally from England, went on to establish his own very successful stonecutting business and sculpture workshops in the Antient Concert Rooms in Pearse Street. By the early twentieth century his was one of the leading firms in the city.

Some stone carvers were naturally talented, others produced only routine work that was nonetheless very good. Most stonemasons and sculptors had their own favourite tools, which they often made themselves and kept permanently sharp. Theirs was an important and respected craft in eighteenth- and nineteenth-century Dublin. But the twentieth century saw the introduction of concrete into architecture, and the simultaneous evolution of modernist style reduced most stone carvers to making gravestones.

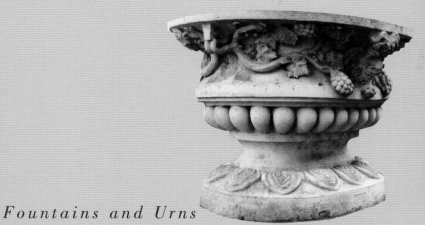

Fountains and Urns

Fountains were a significant feature of ancient Rome. They not only provided its citizens with clean water but were also decorative and graceful additions to the city. The presence of fountains in towns and cities right through the Middle Ages, and indeed on into modern times, was considered to be an important symbol of civilisation itself.

In eighteenth- and nineteenth-century Dublin, fountains were provided in the city for the benefit of the general public and to supply horses with fresh drinking water. A favourite design was the wall niche, which saw the water issue forth from the mouth of a lion into a large basin, or trough. Parts of Dublin had a piped water supply in the early eighteenth century, and there was a basin or reservoir near the present James's Street.

The reverence of the Romans for fountains of fresh water and the lengths to which they went in order to supply it meant that fountains provided an opportunity for creating sculptured memorials. The Rutland Fountain on Merrion Square, dating from the 1790s, was erected in this spirit. Decorative panels and urns made of Coade stone (*see* illustrations, p.51) were used to ornament it. Another such example is the wall fountain at the Rates Office on Lord Edward Street. It is a fine cut-stone and marble composition, which was once equipped with an iron drinking-cup attached to it by a chain. Similar cups were provided on the Victoria Fountain in Dun Laoghaire, erected in 1901 (*see* illustration, p.21).

The Victorian period saw the widespread use of cast iron for fountains, which allowed more inventive designs. The fountains in St Stephen's Green are a good example, with their water jets disguised as bulrushes. An even more elaborate example is the handsome pair of fountains in the People's Park, Dun Laoghaire, which are composed of tiered bowls with four cherubs decorating the base.

Opposite page: A delightful detail from one of the cast-iron fountains in the People's Park in Dun Laoghaire. The ironwork was made in the Sun Foundry in Glasgow in 1895.

This page

Top right: One of the remarkable chimney pots on the roof of the Casino at Marino, carved in 1758 in the form of a funereal urn by Simon Vierpyl.

Above: This Victorian fountain from St Stephen's Green cleverly disguises its water jets as bulrushes.

Bottom right: A *campana* or bell-shaped urn with figures representing horsemen, from the now-vanished Victorian house, Scotch Rath, in Dalkey. The urn was part of a memorial.

Bottom left: A large, late nineteenth-century funereal urn, which now stands in front of the RDS in Ballsbridge, came originally from Gibbstown House in County Meath. The tall urn, with its scroll handles in the form of swans, is based on a design by Bertel Thorwaldsen.

Top left: A massive stucco urn at Stewart's Hospital in Palmerstown is part of the elaborate Victorian alterations which were made when it was converted from a private house into a hospital in 1894.

Above: The Phoenix Column in the Phoenix Park is one of the most handsome pillars in Ireland, set as it is on a stepped pedestal. It was erected by Lord Chesterfield, the lord lieutenant of Ireland, in 1745 to commemorate, among other things, the new long, straight avenue that runs through the park.

Opposite page

Top left: This rustic arch is part of an unusual bridge over a stream at Glensouthwell, near Danesmote in Rathfarnham. It was typical of the eighteenth-century fashion for rustic buildings to have such features in estates and parkland.

Top right: An attractive temple that overlooks the lake at Luttrellstown Castle, providing an elegant front to an eighteenth-century plunge bath.

Bottom right: This garden pavilion at Montebello in Killiney is typical of the many summer houses and gazebos which were built in Victorian times.

Gazebos and Follies

Follies have been defined as 'foolish monuments to greatness and great monuments to foolishness.' A gazebo, or folly, is an uncertain category of building that is generally assumed to serve no particular function. However, most of these structures, while providing ample scope for all forms of decorative architecture, did have a purpose. A few examples have been included here because they are so ornamental and because those which remain in the Dublin region, at least, are now considered to be important landmarks.

The Casino at Marino could be described as a giant-sized folly. It has all the requisites of a salubrious permanent dwelling, but was only ever used as an elegant summer house by Lord Charlemont. One of the best examples is the extraordinary Bottle Tower in Churchtown, which is perhaps one of the most unusually shaped buildings in Ireland. It is a conical tower with a winding staircase meandering up the side of it, hugging the outer wall. One might think it was built for the sheer fun of it, yet it served a useful purpose as a barn for storing grain and also had a pigeon house attached.

The designers and builders of follies took Roman temples, columns, Gothic arches, ancient pyramids, towers, obelisks and grottoes as sources of inspiration. Some were designed purely for

ornament, to create an eye-catching feature in a landscape or parkland, while others served as monuments and bore inscriptions to the memory of some loved one, or animal. The Stillorgan obelisk on Carysfort Avenue, for instance, is an extravagant monument that was designed and built in 1727 in memory of Lady Allen.

On occasion, follies were built for the purpose of providing employment during times of hardship, such as the famine of 1741 and the Great Famine of 1845–1850. The Killiney obelisk was built partly to ornament the deer park of its owner, John Mapas, but also, as its inscription records, to assist the poor: 'Last year being hard on the poor, the walls about these hills and this erected by John Mapas esq. June 1742.'

Garden pavilions and viewing towers were popular ornaments in private grounds in the nineteenth century, and there are many good examples of these in well-to-do residential districts, such as Killiney. In fact, garden architecture is a subject in its own right, with a great variety of rustic summer houses, shell grottoes and boat houses to be found throughout the country.

Conservatories

While most surviving conservatories are of nineteenth-century date, the idea of an orangery or glazed room attached to the house had been fashionable since the Georgian period. The Victorian taste for adding conservatories to houses was fuelled by an increasing interest in hot-house plants and gardening, and also by the availability of cast iron as a building material. At that time, every house of a reasonable size would have been equipped with one or more glasshouses, and perhaps a conservatory.

At Cabinteely House, for instance, there is a large range of glasshouses, in which vegetables, flowers, grapes and possibly peaches and melons were all grown. The glasshouse and gardens have now been restored by Dun Laoghaire–Rathdown County Council.

Part of a stone-built orangery with an arcade and columns survives at Brackenstown House in Swords. While these Georgian structures were quite architectural, the Victorian models were more delicate and elaborate, usually supported by thin cast-iron columns and decorated with finials and other ornament.

The conservatory, a light, airy space that was usually very warm, added an extra room and provided a transition between the house and the garden, where ferns and other exotic plants were grown. In England, the removal of a tax on glass in 1857 also encouraged the development of larger and more ornate conservatories. An elaborate cast-iron conservatory at Clontra in Shankill, with its decorative iron finials and Gothic detail, is a good example of the ornate Victorian style. Floors were usually decorated with tiles, and sometimes coloured glass was used, as at Gortmore in Dundrum.

Index